An Introduction to Windows 7

by

P.R.M. Oliver

and

N. Kantaris

Bernard Babani (publishing) Ltd
The Grampians
Shepherds Bush Road
London W6 7NF
England

www.babanibooks.com

Please Note

Although every care has been taken with the production of this book to ensure that any projects, designs, modifications and/or programs, etc., contained herewith, operate in a correct and safe manner and also that any components specified are normally available in Great Britain, the Publishers and Author(s) do not accept responsibility in any way for the failure (including fault in design) of any project, design, modification or program to work correctly or to cause damage to any equipment that it may be connected to or used in conjunction with, or in respect of any other damage or injury that may be so caused, nor do the Publishers accept responsibility in any way for the failure to obtain specified components

Notice is also given that if equipment that is still under warranty is modified in any way or used or connected with home-built equipment then that warranty may be void.

© 2009 BERNARD BABANI (publishing) LTD

First Published - November 2009

British Library Cataloguing in Publication Data:

A catalogue record for this book is available from the British Library

ISBN 978 0 85934 706 8

Cover Design by Gregor Arthur

Printed and bound in Great Britain for Bernard Babani (publishing) Ltd

About this Book

An Introduction to Windows 7 was written for you if you want to quickly explore the workings of Microsoft's new Windows operating system. Windows 7 manages the available resources of your computer and 'controls' the programs that run on it. To get the most from your computer it is important that you have a good working knowledge of Windows 7.

The book is produced in full colour and covers the Windows 7 environment with its many windows, boxes and other controls. It explains as simply as possible: how to organise your files, folders and photos; how to use Internet Explorer 8 for your Web browsing and how to obtain, install and use Microsoft Live Mail for your e-mails; how to control your PC and keep it healthy; and how to use Windows 7's Accessibility features if you have poor eyesight or have problems using the keyboard or mouse.

The material in the book is presented using everyday language, avoiding jargon as much as possible. It was written with the non technical, non computer literate person in mind. It is hoped that with its help you will be able to get the most out of your computer when using Windows 7, and that you will be able to do it in the shortest, most effective and enjoyable way. Most of all, have fun!

About the Authors

Phil Oliver graduated in Mining Engineering at Camborne School of Mines and has specialised in most aspects of surface mining technology, with a particular emphasis on computer related techniques. He has worked in Guyana, Canada, several Middle Eastern and Central Asian countries, South Africa and the United Kingdom, on such diverse projects as: the planning and management of bauxite, iron, gold and coal mines; rock excavation contracting in the UK; international mining equipment sales and international mine consulting. He later took up a lecturing position at Camborne School of Mines (part of Exeter University) in Surface Mining and Management. He has now retired, to spend more time writing (www.philoliver.com) and developing Web sites.

Noel Kantaris graduated in Electrical Engineering at Bristol University and after spending three years in the Electronics Industry in London, took up a Tutorship in Physics at the University of Queensland. Research interests in Ionospheric Physics, led to the degrees of M.E. in Electronics and Ph.D. in Physics. On return to the UK, he took up a Post-Doctoral Research Fellowship in Radio Physics at the University of Leicester, and then a lecturing position in Engineering at the Camborne School of Mines, Cornwall, (part of Exeter University), where he was also the CSM Computing Manager. At present he is IT Director of FFC Ltd.

Trademarks

Microsoft, **Windows**, **Windows 7**, **Windows Aero**, **Windows XP**, and **Windows Vista** are either registered trademarks or trademarks of Microsoft Corporation.

All other brand and product names used in the book are recognised as trademarks, or registered trademarks, of their respective companies.

Contents

Using the Windows Key

Using the Windows key ⊞ with the following keyboard shortcuts gives you very quick access to many of Windows 7's features. These are well worth learning as they will save you a lot of time.

⊞	Open or close the **Start** menu.
⊞+⇧	Maximise active window.
⊞+⇩	Restore or Minimise active window.
⊞+⇐	Snap active window to left.
⊞+⇒	Snap active window to right.
⊞+*n*	Open the *nth* program on the Taskbar.
⊞+Pause	Opens the **System** Properties box.
⊞+B	Move focus to the **Notification** area.
⊞+D	Toggle showing the Desktop.
⊞+E	Open Computer window.
⊞+F	Search for a file or folder.
⊞+G	Show and cycle through gadgets.
⊞+L	Lock your computer, or switch users.
⊞+M	Minimise all windows to the Taskbar.
⊞+Shift+M	Restore minimised windows.
⊞+P	Set second monitor or projector display.
⊞+R	Open the **Run** box.
⊞+T	Cycle through programs on the Taskbar.
⊞+Tab	Cycle through programs on the Taskbar using **Flip 3-D**.
⊞+Space	Show the Desktop using **Aero Peek**.
⊞+U	Open the **Ease of Access Center**.
⊞+X	Open the **Windows Mobility Center**.

A First Look at Windows 7

Windows 7 is Microsoft's new Operating System for PCs. It is the software that manages the available resources of a computer and 'controls' the applications (or programs) that run on it.

Windows 7 is actually what Windows Vista should have been to start with. It is smaller, faster, simpler, and more focused than Vista If you were a fan of Windows Vista, you will love it. If not, then this is the version you've been waiting for, as Microsoft have made changes to almost everything. Technically, Windows 7 is a major upgrade of Vista, but from a usability point of view it is a very major one indeed.

There was a lot of negative media coverage about Vista as an operating system. Actually we both used and liked it, but Windows 7 is much, much better. A lot of prejudice was involved, which should die now with Windows 7.

Windows 7 is available in Europe in four main editions. **Starter**, the cheapest, sold pre-installed on Netbooks. The **Home Premium** edition with extra features, such as Windows Media Centre, Aero Desktop and Windows Touch. The **Professional** edition with extra networking and hardware protection for business users, and the **Ultimate** edition for those who want all the features going.

Unlike Vista, the Windows 7 versions are true supersets of one another. Microsoft have said "As customers upgrade from one version to the next, they keep all features and functionality from the previous edition".

Most home PCs will come with the Home Premium edition pre-loaded and users will almost certainly find that this contains all the facilities they will need. To write this book we have used a version of the Ultimate edition of Windows 7.

The Windows 7 Desktop

When you switch on your PC and enter your user details, Windows 7 opens with the Desktop (or working area of the screen), as shown for our version in Fig. 1.1 below.

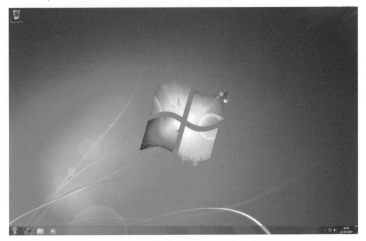

Fig. 1.1 Our Windows 7 Opening Screen

This new Desktop image for Windows 7 is certainly very colourful, but whether you want to look at it every day is another matter. It is very easy to change though, as we cover later in Chapter 7. Microsoft have provided quite a few alternative images, and even some UK photographs.

Notice the completely new **Taskbar** at the bottom of the screen. Some of its new features take a little getting used to, but take it from us, it is worth the effort.

The Taskbar

By default, the **Taskbar** is located at the bottom of the Windows 7 Desktop, but as long as it is not locked (if necessary right-click the **Taskbar** and uncheck the **Lock the Taskbar** option), you can 'drag' it to any border of the screen. In fact with a widescreen monitor the **Taskbar** works very well vertically on the right side of the Desktop.

The **Taskbar** is the area of the Desktop that contains the **Start** button 🌐 on the left, the **Notification Area** and the **Show Desktop** button ▌ on the right, and buttons for all your pinned and open programs, as shown in Fig. 1.2.

Fig. 1.2 The Windows 7 Taskbar

As with previous versions of Windows, when you open a program or window, a button for it is placed on the **Taskbar**. But Windows 7 has no Quick Launch toolbar, you add (or pin) shortcuts straight onto the Taskbar itself.

Fig. 1.3 Windows 7 Taskbar Buttons

So the applications you use most can always be shown on the **Taskbar**, whether they are open or not. Running programs and open windows are shown by buttons with a visible border, whereas 'pinned' shortcuts that are not open, such as Media Player in Fig. 1.3 above, have no borders.

If an item is not open, just clicking its button will open it. You can preview the contents of an open application by hovering the mouse pointer over its button on the **Taskbar**. A thumbnail appears showing a miniature version of the window, which even works if the window has a video or animation playing. In Fig. 1.4 on the next page, we show the preview of what was open in our Internet Explorer at the time.

As you can see, there were three tabs open and each is shown as a thumbnail. Moving the mouse pointer over a thumbnail temporarily displays that window full size on the screen so you can see in more detail what it contains – this is called Aero Peek. Clicking a thumbnail will open the program with that view active, and clicking the Close button ☒ on a thumbnail will close that tab or window. Moving the mouse pointer away will stop the operation with everything left the same.

Fig. 1.4 Thumbnails Showing Open Explorer Tabs

So now, using the **Taskbar**, you can always see what applications you have open, which is the active one, what it contains, and quickly switch between them.

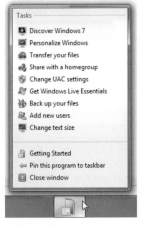

Fig. 1.5 A Windows 7 Jump List

When the **Taskbar** is unlocked you can now drag your **Taskbar** buttons and place them in your preferred order.

If you right-click a **Taskbar** button, a new **Jump List** appears with a list of pre-programmed, or common, actions associated with the clicked object.

In Fig. 1.5 we show this for the Getting Started window, which can be opened from the **Start** menu (Fig. 1.6). The programmed actions associated with the button are shown as **Tasks** at the top of the list. Those at the bottom are available for all program and window buttons, and are all you will see for most applications not specially written with this Windows 7 feature in mind.

The **Pin this program to the taskbar** option is one way to place a shortcut to a program 'permanently' on the **Taskbar**. Another way is to right-click a program or shortcut in the **Start** menu and select the **Pin to Taskbar** option from the context menu that opens (see Fig. 1.15, on page 13).

The Start Button and Menu

 Windows 7 should start up as soon as you switch on your PC, so you don't have to start it manually. Then, clicking the **Start** button 🌐 on the left end of the Taskbar, or pressing the Windows key 🪟, opens the **Start** menu which gives you access to all the applications and settings on your computer. Fig. 1.6 shows a typical **Start** menu, as well as the **Recycle Bin** icon.

Fig. 1.6 The Opening Windows 7 Start Menu with Large Icons

Once you start using Windows 7, the menu in the left pane will have two parts (Fig. 1.7 on the next page). When first used, as shown above, Windows 7 places some useful shortcuts on it. As you use Windows it will automatically replace these with shortcuts to the applications you use most frequently. You can also add (or pin) shortcuts to your most frequently used programs to the top section of the menu. So this section will change as you use your PC.

Windows 7 comes with new versions of **Calculator** 🖩, **Paint** 🎨, **WordPad** 📄 and **Media Centre** ⊙. You can have fun with these, but we don't have the space for them here.

In the pane on the right are shortcuts to Documents, Pictures, Music, Games, Computer, Control Panel, etc., which are normally common to all users.

Just one left-click with your mouse on any of the shortcuts on the **Start** menu will open the application or process.

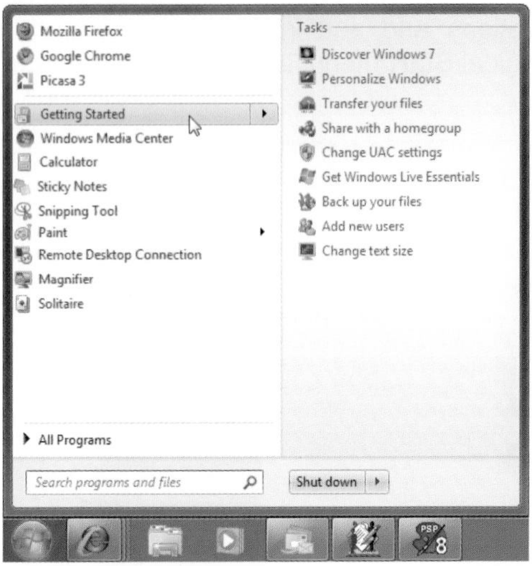

Fig. 1.7 Start Menu (Small Icons) with a Jump List Open

The Windows 7 **Start** menu also supports the **Jump Lists** that we saw earlier. As shown in Fig. 1.7 above, the list appears on the right side of the **Start** menu. According to Microsoft, the new **Start** menu is also touch-friendly, but we don't have the hardware to check this out.

The Notification Area

This is the area, also called the **System Tray**, on the right of the Taskbar that includes a digital clock and date, as well as icons showing the status of the Action Center ⚐, power 🔋 (for a laptop), network 🖳 or ⫽, and the volume setting of your speakers ◁꜏. Other application icons are hidden by default and their notifications are suppressed.

When you click an icon, an information bubble opens showing the status for that setting. Clicking the **Network** icon, for instance, displays information about whether you are connected to a network, as shown in Fig. 1.8.

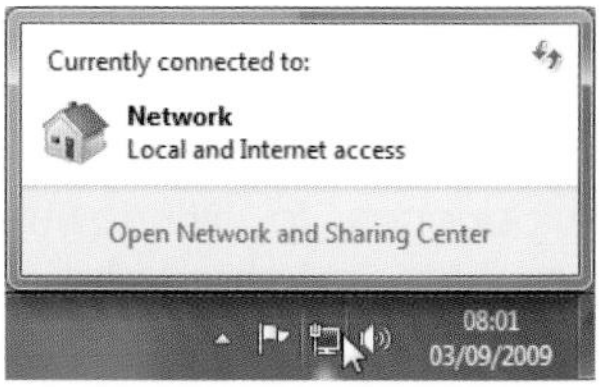

Currently connected to:

Network
Local and Internet access

Open Network and Sharing Center

08:01
03/09/2009

Fig. 1.8 Network Icon

Try clicking the **Volume** icon to open the volume controls so you can control the loudness of the speakers attached to your PC, or built into your laptop.

Clicking the **Action Center** icon (new to Windows 7) gives you a quick view of the status of your PC, as shown in Fig. 1.9. If any problems are shown, you can click the **Open Action Center** link to find out what they are and hopefully how you can solve them.

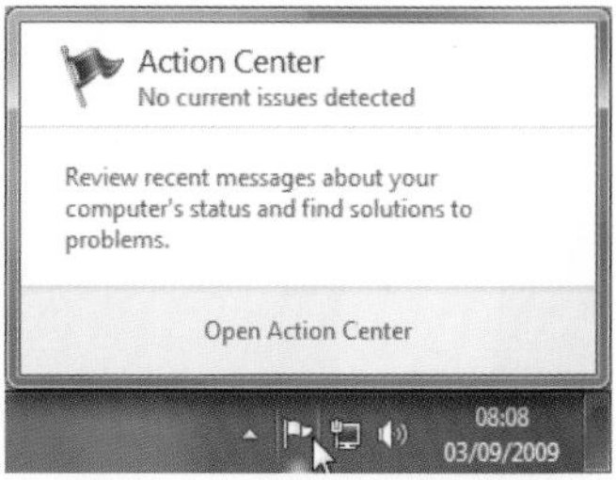

Action Center
No current issues detected

Review recent messages about your computer's status and find solutions to problems.

Open Action Center

08:08
03/09/2009

Fig. 1.9 The Action Center

By default, Windows 7 places any other icons in a 'hidden' area, but you can click the **Show hidden icons** button to temporarily show them again (Fig. 1.10).

If you don't like this default arrangement you can click the **Customize** link and select which icons and notifications appear on your **Taskbar**.

Customize...

Fig. 1.10

The Show Desktop Button

The **Show desktop** button ▍ is now on the right-hand end of the **Taskbar** and has two functions. Hovering your pointer over it temporarily closes all your open windows and lets you see any gadgets or icons you have on your Desktop – this is called Aero Peek. When clicked it acts as the **Show desktop** button and minimises all open windows to the **Taskbar**. Clicking it again re-opens the same windows.

Windows Aero

As it did with Vista, 'Windows Aero' gives a strong visual experience to Windows 7. If your PC is capable of 3D graphics you should be able to see and use the new window colours, themes and transparent borders, and get the **Flip 3D** feature, shown in Fig. 1.11, when you hold the 🎴 Window key down and press the**Tab** key. Every time you press the **Tab** key, or rotate the scroll wheel on your mouse, the windows on the screen change position in really spectacular fashion. To open a particular window, point to it and left-click.

Fig. 1.11 Flip 3D in Action

Another way to quickly identify and open the window you want is to use the **Alt+Tab** keys together. This lets you flip through thumbnails of your windows by keeping the **Alt** key depressed and pressing the **Tab** key repeatedly. If you pause on a thumbnail you get an Aero Peek view of its window in the background. Releasing the **Alt** key opens the selected window.

Aero also includes some new features for window management, that don't use the standard window controls, which with higher and higher resolution displays are getting smaller and harder to use.

Aero Shake

Windows 7 includes a unique new way, called **Aero Shake**, to minimise all windows except for the one currently active. You just grab it by the title bar and 'shake vigorously'. This does not always work with older programs. Shaking again will restore the other windows.

Aero Snaps

By dragging open windows in certain ways, you can 'snap' them to the edges of the screen, and maximise, or minimise them. These methods do not work on 'full size' windows.

To **maximise** the current window, drag its title bar up toward the top of the screen. When the cursor touches the top of the screen, the window will maximise.

To **'snap' the current window to the left side** of the screen, drag it to the left. When the cursor hits the left side of the screen, the window will snap to that edge and resize to occupy the left half of the screen (see also Fig. 2.9, page 24).

To **snap to the right side** of the screen, drag the window to the right. When the cursor hits the screen edge, the window will resize and snap to the right half of the screen. These can be used together. If you snap one window to the left and one to the right, you can very easily drag and drop files between them.

To **restore** a maximised or snapped window, simply drag it back towards the centre of the screen and it will return to its previous size and position.

It is very easy to control Aero and Windows 7's other visual features by right-clicking on an empty part of the Desktop and selecting the **Personalize** option from the context menu. This opens the window shown in Fig. 7.6 on page 99, in which you can customise most of Windows 7's features. You can spend many happy hours here! Clicking on **Window Color**, opens the very colourful window shown in Fig. 7.8 for you to play with. You can control the colours of your windows and set whether they are 'transparent' or not. These settings will be altered, though, whenever you select a new **Theme**.

User Accounts

Windows 7 makes it possible for several people to share a computer (a family maybe) with each having their own set-up. This is done using individual User Accounts. Each account tells Windows 7 what files and folders the holder can access, what changes he or she can make to the computer, and controls personal preferences, such as Desktop backgrounds and colour schemes.

At the top of the **Start** menu the name of the current user is displayed with a picture or icon above it, as shown here and in Fig. 1.6. Left-clicking this icon opens the User Accounts window shown in Fig. 1.12.

Fig. 1.12 The User Accounts Window

This is where the person logged on can create or change their user password, choose a different picture or icon, change the name or type of their account, etc.

When you log on to Windows 7, the Welcome screen displays the accounts that are available on the computer. You can make life easier, as we do, by only using one account, but then everyone that uses the PC has the same access to everything. If that isn't a problem this is by far the easiest way to go.

Running Programs

As Windows 7 is an operating system, it manages the other programs you run on your PC, such as word processors, spreadsheets, databases and games. You can double-click a shortcut icon on your Desktop to open a program, but the **Start** menu (Fig. 1.6) is the main way to access your computer's programs, folders, and settings. As we saw on page 5, clicking the **Start** button 🟦 on the left end of the Taskbar, opens the **Start** menu. To open a program shown in the left pane of this menu, just click it. The program opens and the **Start** menu closes.

If the program you want isn't listed but you know its name, just start typing the name into the **Search programs and files** box at the bottom of the left pane.

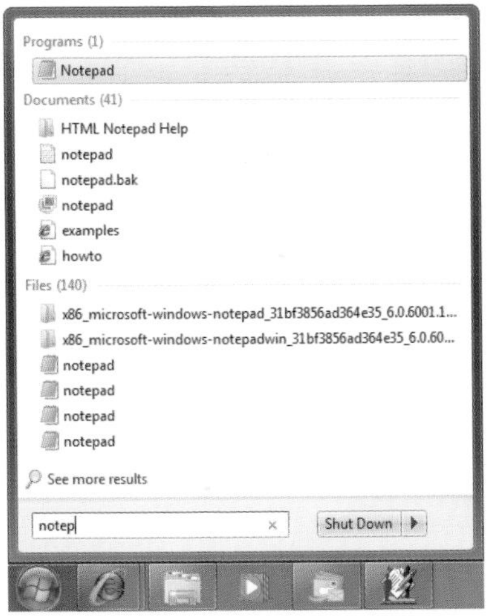

In Fig. 1.13, to open the Notepad text editor, we started typing its name in the **Search** box. The **Start** menu pane instantly displayed search results, right from the first letter typed, and became more selective as each new letter was added.

What we were looking for soon appeared at the top of the list under the **Programs** heading, as shown here. Clicking it opened the Notepad program and closed the **Start** menu.

Fig. 1.13 Searching for a Program

This method saves you having to find the program in a menu, and as the focus starts in the **Search programs and files** box, you don't even need to click it before you start typing.

If all else fails, click **All Programs** above the **Search** box and the left pane will show a long list of programs in alphabetical order, followed by a list of folders, as shown here in Fig. 1.14.

Fig. 1.14 The All Programs List with the Accessories Folder Opened

This shows some of the contents of the **All Programs** list on one of our computers, and the contents of the Windows **Accessories** folder.

As with Vista, in Windows 7, programs are given distinctive icons in these lists. Clicking on the **Notepad** option, starts the program in its own window.

Folders, like the **Accessories** folder, have a different icon and can contain other folders, documents, programs or other items.

To close an opened folder on this list, left-click it again. To get back to the programs you saw when you first opened the **Start** menu, click **Back** at the bottom of the menu (Fig. 1.14).

Changing the Start Menu

As mentioned earlier, the **Start** menu has the ability to adapt the first of its two-column menus to the way you use your PC. It keeps track of what features and programs you use the most and adds them to the list at the bottom of the left column. For example, if you use **WordPad** a couple of times by selecting it from the **Accessories** sub-menu, next time you click the **Start** button you will see this application pinned to the bottom half of the **Start** menu.

Fig. 1.15 Using a Context Menu

This saves time as you don't then have to scroll through menu lists to find the application you want to use.

To remove an application from the left pane of the **Start** menu, right-click it with your mouse and select the option **Remove from this list** from the context menu, as shown in Fig. 1.15. This removes the name of the application from the list, but not the application itself from your hard disc.

You also have the menu options, **Pin to Start Menu** and **Pin to Taskbar**. The first of these adds the program to the top half of the left pane of the **Start** menu which is a more permanent list. The second option pins the selected program to the **Taskbar**, so from then on you will be able to click its button on the **Taskbar** to start the program.

 When some programs are installed on your PC they place a shortcut icon on your Desktop, like that shown here. Right-clicking this, displays similar options to those above, so you can pin the program to either the **Start** menu or the **Taskbar**.

Windows 7 does not place shortcut icons on the lower **Start** menu for programs you have pinned on the **Taskbar**, no matter how many times you use the programs.

As with most things in Windows 7 you can customise the **Start** menu and the **Taskbar** by right-clicking on the **Start** button ● and selecting **Properties**. We will leave it to you to explore the options here. The **Customize** button is a good place to start. This is where we changed the size of the Start menu icons shown earlier in Figs 1.6 and 1.7.

Ending a PC Session

Fig. 1.16 Shut
Down Options

When you have finished for the day, it is important to save your work and 'turn off' your computer properly, both to protect your data and to save energy. With Windows 7 there are several options for ending the session, all available from the **Power** button at the bottom of the **Start** menu as shown in Fig. 1.16. Clicking the **Start** button 🔵 and hovering the pointer over the right arrow button ▶, will open the options menu shown.

From here you can select to **Switch User**, **Log Off** the current user and leave the computer running so another user can log on, **Lock** the Computer so that it needs a password before you can carry on working, **Restart** the computer to clear the memory settings and reset Windows, put the PC in **Sleep** mode, or use **Hibernate** if the option is available.

By default, the **Shut Down** button Shut Down closes the computer completely, but you can change this by right-clicking the **Start** button 🔵 and selecting **Properties**. If there are updates to install, the **Shut Down** button changes to 🔵 Shut Down. When you click it in this form, Windows 7 installs the updates and then shuts down the PC.

If you are a mobile PC user you just have to close the lid, unless you leave your laptop where it could be stolen. In which case it is much safer to shut down completely, so that it does not produce any detectable signal.

In our experience, sleep and hibernation modes often don't seem to work correctly. If this happens on your PC we suggest you go to the Web site:

www.sevenforums.com/tutorials

and click the **Power Management** icon. Good luck, we have solved many of our Power problems here, and more solutions are added all the time.

2

The Windows 7 Environment

In Windows 7 every user starts with a set of data folders called simply **My Documents**, **My Pictures**, **My Music** and **My Videos** stored in **Libraries**. To see your Libraries, click the **Start** button 🔵, then click your log-on name at the top of the **Start** menu (see Fig. 1.6) and click **Libraries** in the left pane. This opens an Explorer window similar to Fig. 2.1 below.

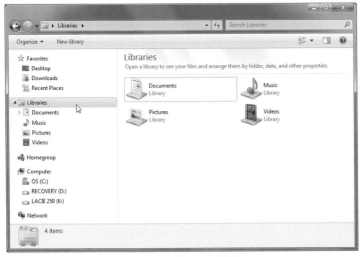

Fig. 2.1 A Set of Personal Libraries

Libraries (see page 28) are new to Windows 7. Although not folders themselves, they can point to different folders on your hard disc, or on an external drive attached to your computer. They let you quickly access files from multiple folders without moving them from their original location. Say you have music files on your hard disc and on an external drive, you can now access all of your music files from the Music library.

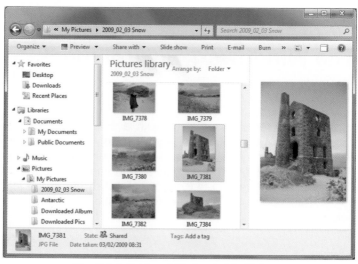

Fig. 2.2 A Folder of Photos in My Pictures

The left pane of the Explorer window, called the **Navigation** pane, lists your **Favorites** and gives you access to tree views of your **Libraries**, your **Computer** and your **Networks**. The right pane lists the folders and files in the selected location.

Clicking a link in the **Navigation** pane opens the contents of that folder in the right pane. Double-clicking a folder in the right pane will open it and display its contents.

In the **Navigation** pane of Fig. 2.2 you can see that the default contents of the **Documents Library** are **My Documents** (your personal documents folder) and **Public Documents** (those available to anyone that uses the computer).

In Fig. 2.2 above, we have clicked on a folder name in the **My Pictures** listing to open it. The photographs in the folder are shown in the centre pane. The right **Preview** pane is opened and closed by clicking the **Preview Pane** button on the toolbar at the top of the window. This shows a larger preview image of whatever is selected in the centre pane.

Parts of a Window

In Fig. 2.3 below we show a typical Windows 7 Explorer window with its constituent parts labelled and later described. By default, menus are not shown in these windows. To see the **Menu** bar in a Windows 7 window, press the **Alt** key, or click the **Organize** button and select **Layout, Menu Bar**.

You may have noticed by now that the buttons on the toolbars of the different Explorer windows change to reflect the type of work you can do in that type of window.

Pictures windows, for example, have a **Slide Show** button, whereas **Music** windows have **Play** and **Play All** buttons.

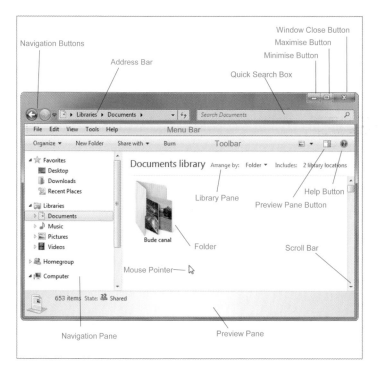

Fig. 2.3 Parts of a Windows 7 Explorer Window

The typical Explorer window is subdivided into several areas which have the following functions:

Area	*Function*
Minimise button	Left-clicking the **Minimise** button stores a window and its contents as an icon on the **Taskbar**. Clicking on such an icon will restore the window.
Maximise button	Left-clicking the **Maximise** button fills the screen with the active window. When that happens, the **Maximise** button changes to a **Restore Down** button which can be used to restore the window to its former size.
Close button	The extreme top right button that you click to close a window.
Navigation buttons	The **Go Back** (left) button takes you to the previous display, while the **Go Forward** (right) button takes you to the next display. The down-arrow gives access to **Recent Pages**.
Address bar	Shows the location of the current folder. You can change locations here, or switch to an Internet Explorer window by typing a Web address (URL).
Quick search box	The box in which you type your search criteria. As you start typing the first few letters, the displayed files filter down to just the matching terms. This makes finding your files much easier.
Menu bar	The bar which only displays if you press the **Alt** key. It allows you to choose from several menu options. Clicking on a menu item displays the pull-down menu associated with it.

Toolbar	A bar of icons that you click to carry out some common actions. The icons displayed on the toolbar depend on the type of window.
Scroll bars/buttons	The bars/buttons at the extreme right and bottom of each window (or pane within a window) that contain a scroll box/button. Clicking on these allows you to see parts of a document that might not be visible in that size window.
Mouse pointer	The arrow which appears when the pointer is placed over menus, scroll bars, buttons, and folder lists.

Window Panes

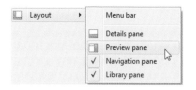

Fig. 2.4 Controlling Panes

With Windows 7's Explorer windows you can control which panes are open by clicking the **Organize** toolbar button, selecting **Layout** from the drop-down menu, and clicking one of the options as shown in Fig. 2.4.

Option	*Function*
Details Pane	To display information on an item.
Preview Pane	To preview the contents of a selected file without opening it.
Navigation Pane	Shows links and folders so that you can easily navigate around your PC.
Library Pane	To manage the contents and view of the Library being looked at.

Menu Bar Options

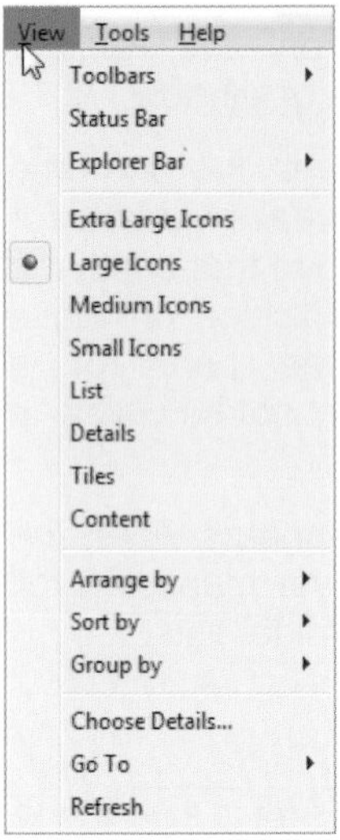

Each window's menu bar option has associated with it a pull-down sub-menu (you can open the menu by pressing the **Alt** key). To activate a menu or sub-menu option, highlight it and click the left mouse button.

Items on the sub-menu marked with an arrow to their right ▶, open up additional options when selected.

Most Windows 7 system applications offer the **File**, **Edit**, **View**, **Tools** and **Help** menu options.

Fig. 2.5 A Typical Windows 7 Sub-menu

Note: Having activated a menu, whether from the menu bar or a right-click, you can close it without taking any further action by simply left-clicking the mouse pointer somewhere else on the screen, or by pressing the **Esc** key.

Dialogue Boxes

Three periods after a sub-menu option or command, means that a dialogue box will open when the option or command is selected. A dialogue box is used for the insertion of additional information.

To see a dialogue box, click the **Start** button and select the **Computer** menu option. If necessary, press the **Alt** key to display the **Menu bar**, click **Tools** and on the drop-down sub-menu select **Folder options**. This opens the Folder Options dialogue box with its General tab selected. In Fig. 2.6 on the next page we show this dialogue box with its View tab selected so that you can see different types of option lists.

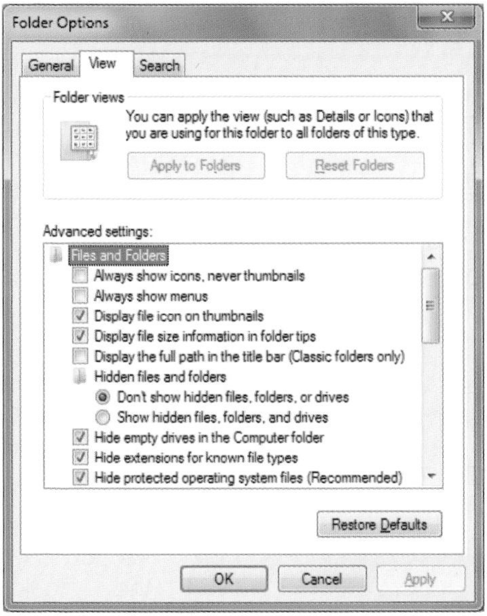

Fig. 2.6 The Folder Options Dialogue Box

When a dialogue box opens, you can use the **Tab** key to move the dotted rectangle, or focus, from one field to another, or more easily, you can use the mouse.

Some dialogue boxes contain List boxes which show a column of available choices. If there are more choices than can be seen in the area provided, use the scroll bars to reveal them, as above.

Dialogue boxes may contain Check boxes ☑, which offer a list of features you can switch on or off. Selected options show a tick in the box against the option name.

Another feature available is the Option, or Radio button ◉, with a list of mutually exclusive items. The default choice is marked with a blue dot. Unavailable options are dimmed.

To cancel a dialogue box, either press the **Cancel** button, or the **Esc** key enough times to close the dialogue box and then the menu system.

Changing the Date and Time

Fig. 2.7 Date and Time
Properties Dialogue Box

On the far right of the **Taskbar** is a digital clock showing the current time as given by the internal clock of your PC. Left-clicking the time display, opens the pop-up window shown in Fig. 2.7. Clicking the **Change date and time settings** link on this opens the **Date and Time** box, so that you can control your clock.

Fig. 2.8 The Date and Time Box

As you can see here, the clock changes automatically between Summer and Winter times.

On the Internet Time tab you can set your clock to synchronise with an Internet time server, so it should always be correct.

On the Additional Clocks tab, you can set to show up to two extra clocks for

different time zones. With a son in Australia, we find this a useful feature. You can view the extra clocks by hovering the pointer over the normal **Taskbar** clock, as shown here. If you click on the **Taskbar** clock, a pop-up window similar to that in Fig. 2.7 opens, but showing all your clocks.

Manipulating Windows

To use any Windows program effectively, you need to be able to work with a series of windows, and make a window active, move it, or re-size it so that you can see all of it.

Changing the active window – If you have several windows open on the screen, you can make one active by simply clicking it with the left mouse button, or, if it is not visible, click its icon on the **Taskbar**.

Moving a window – To move a window (or a dialogue box), point to its title bar with the mouse, and drag it with the left button depressed until it is where you want on the screen, then release the mouse button. You can only do this if the window does not occupy the full screen and it has a maximise button ▫ visible.

Minimising and maximising windows – To minimise a window into a **Taskbar** icon, maybe to free up Desktop space, left-click the **Minimize** button ▬ in the upper-right corner of the window.

   To maximise a window so that it fills the entire screen, left-click the **Maximize** button ▫, or double-click in the title bar. Double-clicking again will restore it.

   A window that has been minimised or maximised can be returned to its original size and position on the screen by either clicking on its **Taskbar** icon to expand it to a window, or clicking on the **Restore Down** button ▣ of a maximised window, to reduce it to its former size.

**Re-sizing a window** – You can change the size of a window with the mouse by first moving the window so that the side you want to change is visible, then placing the mouse pointer on the edge of the window, or on a corner, so that it changes to a two-headed arrow, then dragging this arrow to get the size you want.

Closing a window – Any window can be closed at any time, to save screen space and memory, by left-clicking its **Close** button ▬✖▬.

New Aero Features

Windows 7 also includes some new ways to manipulate windows. These were developed to take advantage of its new Touch features, which if you have touch-sensitive hardware lets you manipulate the screen with your fingers.

Aero Shake lets you minimise all windows except for the one currently active. You just grab the title bar (keeping the left mouse button depressed) and 'shake vigorously' to minimise all the other open windows.

Aero Snaps let you 'snap' windows to the edges of the screen, and maximise, or minimise them. To **maximise** the current window, you drag its title bar up towards the top of the screen. When the cursor touches the top of the screen, the window will maximise.

To **'snap' the current window to the left side** of the screen, drag it to the left. When the cursor hits the left side of the screen, the window will snap to that edge and resize to occupy the left half of the screen.

Fig. 2.9 Snapping a Window to the Left

Fig. 2.9 shows the procedure just before the mouse pointer is released. The gold outline of where the snapped window will go is shown against a very colourful Desktop image.

To **snap to the right side** of the screen, drag the window to the right. When the cursor hits the screen edge and the mouse button is released, the window will resize and snap to the right half of the screen. These can be used together. If you snap one window to the left and one to the right, you can very easily drag and drop files between them.

To **restore** a maximised or snapped window, simply drag it back towards the centre of the screen and it will return to its previous size and position.

When you get used to these new features, they make working with your different application windows a pleasure. To start with though, it can be somewhat disconcerting when a window disappears or suddenly 'takes off on its own'.

Aero Snap is turned on by default in Windows 7, but it is easy to turn it off. To do this, open the **Ease of Access Center** with the ⊞+U keyboard shortcut, click the **Make the mouse easier to use** link, and check **Prevent windows from being automatically arranged when moved to the edged of the screen**. Unchecking will turn it on again.

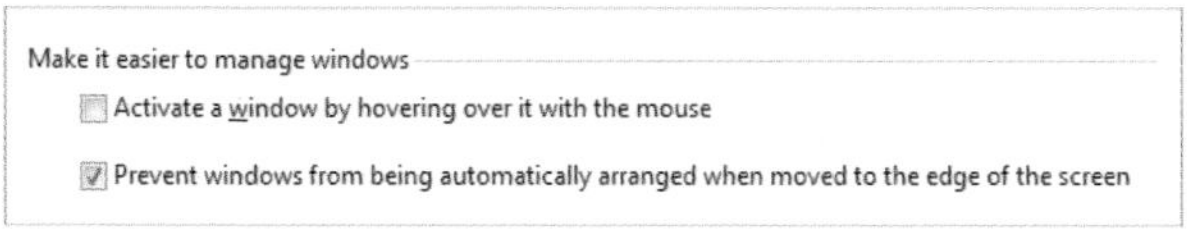

Make it easier to manage windows
- Activate a window by hovering over it with the mouse
- ☑ Prevent windows from being automatically arranged when moved to the edge of the screen

Fig. 2.10 Turning Off the Aero Snap Feature

Help with Windows 7

Whatever you are doing in Windows 7, help is not very far away. Just click the **Start** button 🟦, then click the **Help and Support** menu option to open the main Help window, shown in Fig. 2.11 on the next page.

The **Search Help** text box gives you access to a very powerful Help search facility. Type the word or phrase you want help with into the text box and click the **Search Help** button 🔍. Try it, it's one of our favourite methods.

Fig. 2.11 Windows Help and Support

You can click one of the options in the **Not sure where to start?** section, or use the **Browse Help** button █ to open a browsable list.

When you are in a Windows 7 Explorer window, you can also click the **Get Help** button ⊙ on the toolbar, to get specific help on the type of window you are working with.

As long as you are online, you should make sure the **Online Help** button ⊙ Online Help ▾ is showing at the bottom of the **Help** window. This will ensure you have access to Windows 7's latest Help content. It is a new operating system and Microsoft are updating Help quite frequently.

3

Libraries, Folders and Files

On a computer, a **file** contains related information, such as a word-processed letter, a spreadsheet, a digital photo, a video, or a music track. Windows 7 represents files with icons in its Explorer windows, as shown in Fig. 3.1, so you can tell what kind of file an icon represents just by looking at it.

| Text File | Photo | Word File | Excel File | Video |

Fig. 3.1 File Icons in a Documents Window

You control the size of the icons in the window's **View** sub-menu (page 29). Fig. 3.1 above, shows **Large Icons**.

A **folder** is just a container in which you can store files or other folders. Arranging files into logical groups in folders makes it easier to locate and work with them.

Fig. 3.2 Folders in a My Documents Window

By default, Windows 7 provides four special folders for each user, called **My Documents**, **My Pictures**, **My Music**, and **My Videos** stored in the **C:\Users\Username** folder, as shown in Fig. 3.3 for the 'Username' Phil.

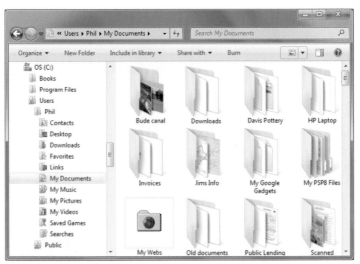

Fig. 3.3 The Default User Folder Structure

Libraries

In Windows 7 you can still open and use these special folders, but now the best way to access the files stored in them is from one of the libraries (see page 15). All of which can be accessed from the **Start** menu. Each Library has a default location to store saved files. In the **Documents** Library, for example, it is the **My Documents** folder. We

recommend that you carry on with this structure, so that photos and folders created for photos would go in the **My Pictures** folder, word processor and spreadsheet files and folders would go in the **My Documents** folder, etc.

In this way, when you click the **Start** button 🔵, the Libraries will be available for you on the top-right of the **Start** menu, as shown here.

You can change how your file and folder icons appear in Windows 7's Explorer windows with the **Views** 'slider' menu on the toolbar of every folder, shown open in Fig. 3.4 below.

Open the folder you want to change. Click the down-arrow next to the **Views** button on the toolbar and move the slider to change the appearance of the icons.

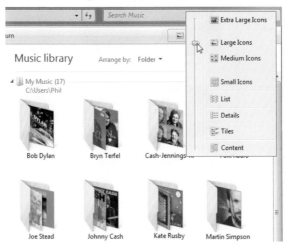

Fig. 3.4 Changing the Size of File and Folder Icons

As shown above, the slider has eight rest positions between **Content** (a new option) and **Extra Large Icons**. You can fine-tune the size of the icons by moving the slider to any point between these positions. As you do this, keep your eye on the **Views** button itself. It changes to show the currently selected view. Very neat.

The Library Pane (see page 19) in each Library window has two controls. The **Includes**: setting lets you manage the locations included in the Library. Clicking the blue link to the right opens the **Library Locations** box in which you can add and remove folders to or from the Library, and change the **Default save location**.

The **Arrange by:** setting lets you filter all the files in the Library and arrange them in various ways, as shown in Fig. 3.5. These vary depending on the type of Library.

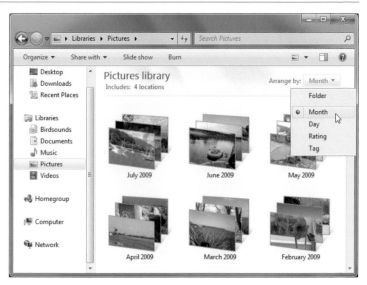

Fig. 3.5 Arranging the Library Contents

Creating a New Folder

To create a new folder in a Library, select **Folder** in the **Arrange by:** section of the **Library Pane**, open the folder you want it to be in, and left-click the **New Folder** toolbar button.

When Windows 7 creates a new folder it gives it the very original name **New Folder**, places it alphabetically in the list of existing items, and highlights the name ready for you to rename it, as shown here. You just type a new name for the folder.

Perhaps an easier way to create a new folder is to go to the location, or folder, where you want to create it, right-click a blank area in the window, select **New**, **Folder** from the context menu, type a name for the new folder, and press **Enter**. This is the way we usually do it.

To rename a file or folder, first select it, then left-click in the name area to select the old name and just type the new name.

Searching for Files and Folders

Windows 7 has a facility to instantly **Search programs and files** on your computer. This appears on the **Start** menu, immediately above the **Start** button 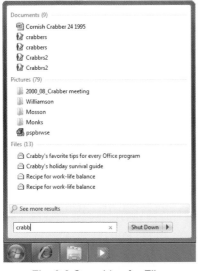, and in every Explorer type window. To locate programs, files, e-mail messages, and other items on your PC just type a file name, a property, or some of the text in a file, and **Search** should quickly find and open it for you.

To find a specific file or folder located anywhere on your PC, open the **Start** menu and start typing in the **Search programs and files** box. As you type, the pane instantly displays search results, right from the first letter typed, with the list becoming more selective as each new letter is added. The results are listed in categories as shown in our example in Fig. 3.6.

If the file or folder you want is listed, simply click it to open it.

If not, you can click the **See more results** link at the bottom of the list, to open the search in a Search Folder as shown in Fig. 3.7, on the next page.

Fig. 3.6 Searching for Files

With Windows 7 you can use the **Save search** button on the toolbar to save the search criteria you have used together with the search results in the **Searches** folder in your Users section (as shown in Fig. 3.3 on page 28). Double-clicking this saved search in the future, will start a new search of the same type.

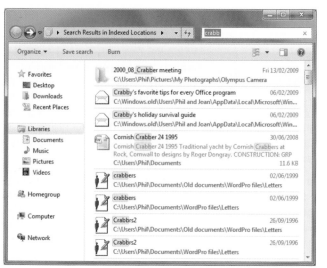

Fig. 3.7 Results in a Search Folder

If you know what folder a file is in, you can open it and use the **Quick Search** box in the folder window to carry out your search in the same way.

Search   🔍

Working with Files and Folders

The longer you work with a computer the more files and folders you accumulate. To keep things manageable you need at least to be able to copy, move and delete them.

Selecting Files and Folders – In Windows you have to select an item before you can do something with it. When it is selected in Windows 7, a file or folder is given a pale blue surround, as shown in Fig. 3.8 on the facing page.

To select one file or folder in a window just click it. To select several you have three main options:

• If they form a contiguous list, left-click the first in the list, then with the **Shift** key depressed, click the last in the list.

Fig. 3.8 A Random Selection of Files and Folders

- To select random objects, as above, hold the **Ctrl** key down and left-click them, one by one.

- To select all the items in a window just use the **Ctrl+A** keyboard shortcut.

To cancel a selection, click in an empty area of the window.

Copying Files and Folders – When you *copy* a file or folder to somewhere else, the original version of the folder or file is not altered or removed, but when you *move* a folder or file to a new location, the original is actually deleted.

To copy selected items into another folder, right-click them and choose the **Copy** option from the shortcut menu. They are then copied to the Windows **Clipboard** which is a temporary storage area in memory where text, graphics and files are stored with the Windows **Cut** and **Copy** commands.

All you need to do now is navigate to the destination folder, right-click in it and select the **Paste** option from the context, or shortcut menu that opens.

Moving Files and Folders – To move selected items into a target folder, choose the **Cut** option from the shortcut menu. This removes them from their current place and copies them to the Windows **Clipboard** so that you can **Paste** them into the target folder.

Using Drag and Drop – If you are happy using the mouse, you can drag selected objects in one folder or between two open folders, with the **Ctrl** key depressed, to copy them.

If you don't use the **Ctrl** key you will move them. You need to be careful with this method though, as it is easy to drop your precious files and folders in the wrong location. You then have to spend 'hours' looking for them!

Creating Desktop Shortcuts – With Windows you can put a shortcut to any program file or document on your Desktop or in a folder. Shortcuts are quick ways to get to the items you use often; they save you having to dig into menus to access them.

The easiest way to do this is to find the program in the **Start**, **All Programs** list and drag it to the Desktop with the right mouse button depressed. When the mouse button is released, select the **Create shortcuts here** option from the menu that opens. This places the new shortcut on the Desktop and you can drag it to the location on your screen that you want. Fig. 3.9 below shows the sequence graphically for creating a shortcut to the WordPad program.

Double-clicking a shortcut icon on the Desktop is much easier than digging deep into the menus to open a program.

Fig. 3.9 Creating a Shortcut on the Desktop

Deleting Files or Folders – To delete or remove files or folders, first select them in an Explorer window, and then either select the **Organize**, **Delete** ✗ Delete   option, right-click them and select **Delete**, or press the **Del** key on the keyboard. All of these methods open a message box giving you the chance to abort the operation by selecting **No**.

Deleting a single folder or file displays a dialogue box similar to that shown in Fig 3.10.

Fig. 3.10 The Delete Folder Warning Box

In any of these cases, to carry on with the deletion select the **Yes** option.

Perhaps now is the time to do some housekeeping and delete any duplicate or unwanted image files. Take care though and make sure you really don't want them! Do carry out this suggestion as we need to demonstrate what happens to deleted items next.

The Recycle Bin

As you can see from the **Delete Folder** message box above, by default all files or folders deleted from a hard disc, are actually placed in a holding folder named the **Recycle Bin**.

If you open the **Recycle Bin**, by double-clicking its Desktop icon, shown here, you will see that it is just a special folder. It lists all the files, folders, Recycle Bin icons and shortcuts that have been deleted from fixed drives since it was last emptied, as shown in Fig. 3.11 on the next page.

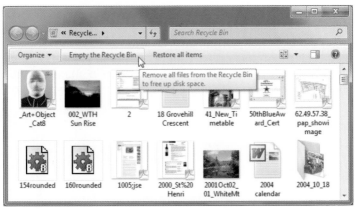

Fig. 3.11 Emptying the Recycle Bin

Windows 7 keeps a record of the original locations of the deleted files and folders, so that it can restore them if necessary. To restore all the items in the **Recycle Bin**, click the **Restore all items** button. To finally delete its contents click the **Empty the Recycle Bin** option pointed to above. Beware though, you won't be able to get the data back again.

To restore specific files or folders, first select them, then click the **Restore selected items** button. To delete an item, select it and press the **Delete** keyboard key.

Every now and then you should open the **Recycle Bin** and delete unwanted files or folders to free up hard disc space.

Sorting and Filtering

As long as you are in Details view, you can control what files are displayed in an Explorer window (filtering) and in what order (sorting). You do this by clicking the headings above the file list.

Just clicking a header will sort the displayed files based on the header. The **Name** header sorts alphabetically, **Size** sorts by file size, etc. Clicking the header again reverses the sort order. In Fig. 3.12 we sorted the files alphabetically by clicking the **Name** header, as shown. Folders are sorted first in the listing, followed by files.

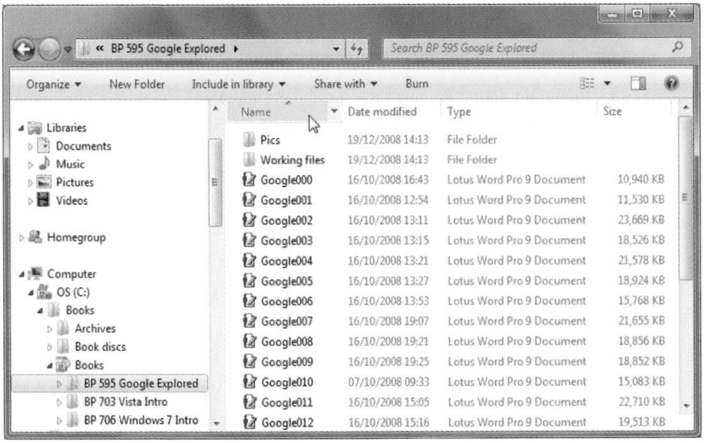

Fig. 3.12 A Folder Sorted by Name

You filter your files when you only want ones with a particular property to be displayed. You do this by clicking the arrow to the right of the heading that you want to filter by. The drop-down menu that opens, depends on the heading clicked. In Fig. 3.13 for instance, you can select to only show files that were last modified in a certain date range, by clicking the arrow to the right of the **Date modified** heading, and selecting the date range in the 'calendar box', or by ticking the boxes next to the types you want.

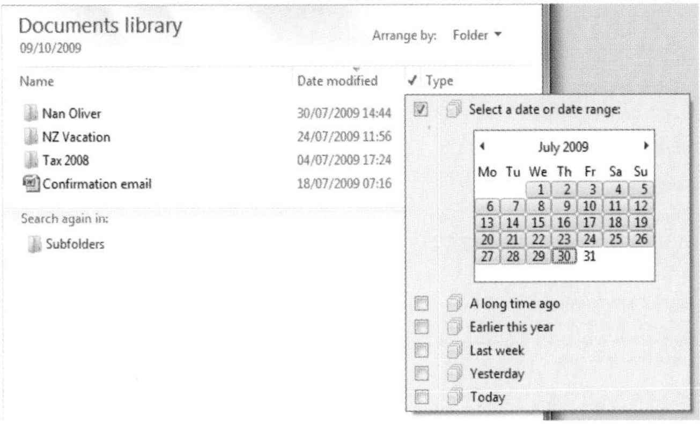

Fig. 3.13 Date Filtering a Folder

Copying to a CD or DVD

To copy files or folders to a CD or DVD, you will need a disc recorder fitted to your PC and a supply of suitable discs.

By default, Windows 7 uses the **Live File System** format for burning CDs and DVDs. With this format you can copy selected files immediately and as often as you want straight to the disc in the recorder drive, just like a USB flash drive or floppy disc. BUT, the discs produced are only compatible with Windows XP, Vista and Windows 7.

To start the process, locate and select the files or folders you want to copy to disc. Make sure that they do not exceed 650 MB for a standard CD or 4.7 GB for a standard DVD. Click the **Burn** button Burn on the Explorer window toolbar, as shown earlier in Fig. 3.8. A balloon message may open on the Taskbar as shown in Fig. 3.14, or you may just be asked to **Insert a disc**.

Fig. 3.14 A CD Burn Notification Message

If you insert a blank recordable or rewritable CD or DVD in the recorder when asked, the format procedure will start. Type a title in the **Burn a Disc** box that opens (Fig. 3.15).

When you click the **Next** button, Windows will format the disc after first checking with you. This took a few minutes for us with a new CD-RW disc. A DVD would take longer. But it only needs doing once.

Fig. 3.15 Preparing a Blank Disc

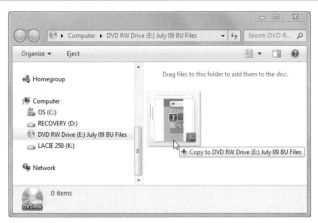

Fig. 3.16 Burning Selected Files to a New CD

When the formatting is complete a new Explorer window opens onto the CD drive. You simply drag the selected files into this as shown in Fig. 3.16. The burning process is then started and the selected files are copied to the disc. You can leave the disc in the drive while you are working and copy more files to it, or delete files from it, whenever you want. This method is useful for making manual backup type copies of your data.

Playing Media Files

 Windows 7 comes with an excellent new version of Windows Media Player, which by default, is used to play your audio and video files (music and films).

Selecting a video file in the Videos Library or an audio file in the Music Library and clicking the **Play** button [▶ Play], will open the file and play it in a Media Player window (Fig. 3.17). Double-clicking the file name will also do this.

Clicking the **Play all** button [Play all] in the Music Library will add all the tracks in the current folder to a Play List and start playing them all in the Media Player.

Fig. 3.17 Playing a Music Track with Media Player

Moving the pointer over the Media Player window opens the player controls, as shown in Fig. 3.18. We don't have the space to go further here, but you should really have fun finding your way around this superb feature.

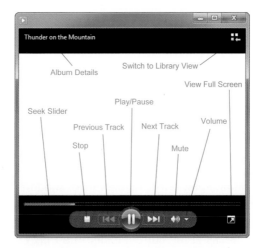

Fig. 3.18 Windows Media Player Controls

Photographs

As we have seen, in Windows 7 the **Pictures Library** points to the **My Pictures** folder provided for storing all of your digital pictures. It is the default location for saving pictures and importing them from your digital camera or scanner. We put most of our images in sub-folders of the **My Pictures** folder, as it makes it easier to keep track of them. The folder below holds some splendid photos from the US Antarctic Program Web Portal of the National Science Foundation.

Fig. 3.19 A Folder of Photos

You should have noticed by now that the toolbar buttons change depending on what you are doing. Fig. 3.19 shows a typical **Pictures** folder toolbar with no files selected. As soon as you select a file, the buttons on the bar are changed, as shown below.

Organize ▼   ⬚ Preview ▼   Share with ▼   Slide show   Print   E-mail   Burn

Fig. 3.20 An Extended Pictures Folder Toolbar

We have already used the **Organize**, **Views** and **Burn** buttons, so perhaps it's time we had a look at some of the other toolbar options.

Printing Photos

Selecting pictures and clicking the **Print** button ⌜Print⌝, displays the **Print Pictures** window shown below.

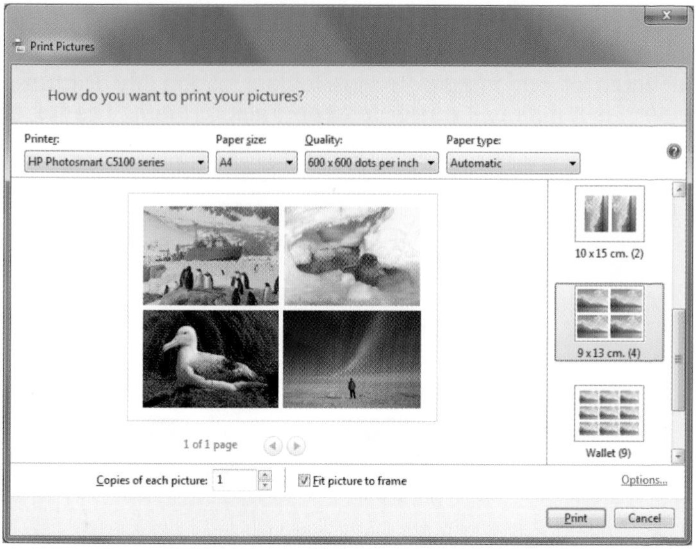

Fig. 3.21 Printing Photos from an Explorer Window

From here you can select the **Printer** to be used, **Paper size**, **Quality** of print, **Paper Type** and a variety of layouts for your pictures. All you have to do then is click the **Print** button.

Slide Show

Clicking the **Slide show** button ⌜Slide show⌝ starts a full-screen slide show of any selected photos or videos in the current folder. You close, or control the show, from its right-click menu shown in Fig. 3.22.

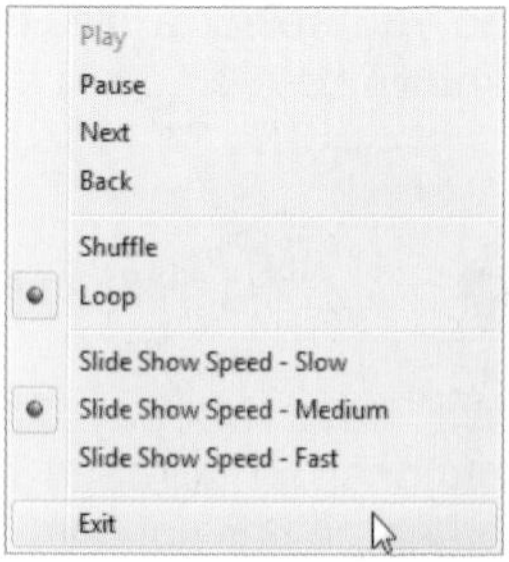

Fig. 3.22 Slide Show Controls

The Windows Photo Viewer

By default, double-clicking a picture in an Explorer folder, or clicking the **Preview** toolbar button , opens the **Windows Photo Viewer**, as shown in Fig. 3.23.

Fig. 3.23 A Mauritius Sunset in the Windows Photo Viewer

The Toolbar at the top of this window offers similar options to those of the original Explorer window. You can use the controls at the bottom to navigate through the current folder, view the pictures in your folder as a slide show, zoom in or out, rotate the image, and delete it from your hard disc.

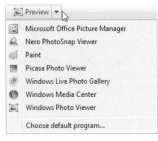

Fig. 3.24 Program Options

Clicking the **Open** button, or the down-arrow ▼ next to the **Preview** button of an Explorer window, opens a list of programs available for editing your photo files.

Windows Live Essentials

Windows 7 does not come packaged with a program for handling and editing photographs. But Microsoft has made **Windows Live Essentials** available as an optional download. This includes a number of new versions of applications designed to work with Windows 7, including **Windows Live Photo Gallery**. Please see Chapter 5 for details of how to carry out the download.

Fig. 3.25 Windows Live Photo Gallery

With the **Windows Live Photo Gallery** you can view (Fig. 3.25), edit and sort your photos and display them in different ways: by date, using star ratings, or using descriptive tags. Once your photos have been fixed and organised, you can save a folder of photos to a blank CD or DVD, or click a button to make a slide show with **Windows Live Movie Make**r. More exploration required here! You could even look for our book BP710 *An Introduction to Windows Live Essentials*.

4

Using the Internet

The Internet links many millions of computers around the world and has revolutionised how we get information and use our computers. How did we ever manage without it? Amongst the many facilities available are browsing the Web and using e-mail to keep in contact with family and friends.

Once you are connected to the Internet you can send e-mail messages to anyone with an e-mail address anywhere in the world. Its free and almost instant. No wonder it's so popular. If you are like us, almost the first thing you do every day is check your e-mail!

The Web (or World Wide Web to use its full name) consists of millions of web sites which give a magazine-like view of almost everything you can think of, but with sound and video as well.

You view the Web with a Web browser, and when Windows 7 is first installed, Microsoft's Internet Explorer 8 is installed with it. That is what we will briefly cover in this chapter, but you can install and use another Web browsing program if you prefer.

Internet Explorer 8

 To start **Internet Explorer**, either click its icon on the **Taskbar** , or click **Start**, **All Programs**, and select **Internet Explorer** Internet Explorer from the **Start** menu. Either of these options, opens Microsoft's Internet browser. The first time you do this, you will probably be stepped through the process of establishing a connection to the Internet.

There are three ways of doing this; **Wireless**, **Broadband**, or **Dial-up**. For a **Wireless** connection you need a wireless router or a network. For a **Broadband** connection you need a broadband modem, also called DSL (Digital Subscriber Line), or a cable modem. For the slowest option, a **Dial-up** connection, you will need a modem. We think most people these days use a wireless router.

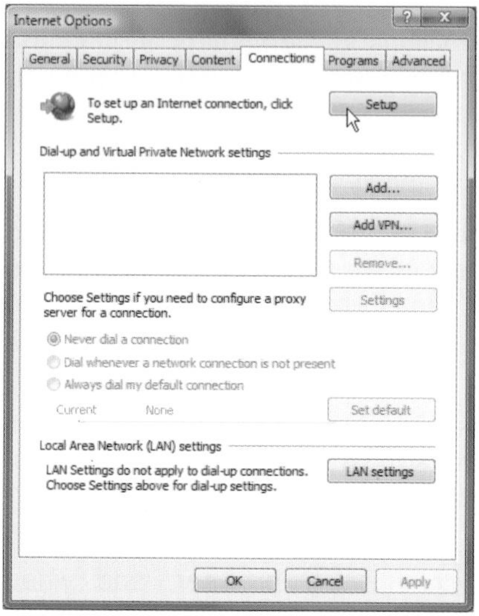

Fig. 4.1 Starting Connection Setup

Whichever method you select you will need to subscribe to an Internet Service Provider (ISP) and you might have to purchase additional hardware. Normally, ISPs provide you with a CD which automates the setup process, but you could also use the **Tools** toolbar icon in Internet Explorer. Select **Internet Options** from the drop-down menu and click the **Setup** button on the Connections tab sheet, as shown here in Fig. 4.1.

However, before starting this operation be sure to find out from your ISP, exactly what settings you will need to enter. They usually send you a letter or e-mail with these details.

The first time you manage to access the Web you will probably get a page supplied by Microsoft or your Service Provider. But you can control what Web page is displayed when you start **Explorer** (called your Home page), in the **General** settings sheet opened with the **Tools**, **Internet Options** menu command. Select **Use current** to make any currently open page your home page, or **Use blank** to show a clear window whenever you start **Explorer**.

Searching the Web

There are many millions of Web pages to look at on the Web, so where do you start? Our favourite place is Google, so let's take a quick look. Start **Explorer**, if it is not already going, log onto the Internet (this is done automatically with broadband), then type **www.google.co.uk** into the **Address** bar (see Fig. 4.3), and press the **Enter** key on the keyboard, or click the **Go to** button → to the right of the address bar.

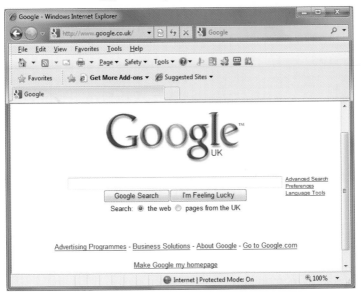

Fig. 4.2 The Google UK Search Page

If all is well and your connection is good you should see Google UK's search page, as in Fig. 4.2. Bear in mind that this (and other Web site screens in the book) may be different at the time you access them. Google especially, like to change their opening logos often and particularly for special events.

Moving the mouse over the underlined links, and some graphics on the page, changes the pointer to a hand 🖑. Clicking the hand pointer, jumps you to different parts of the Web site, or to other sites. This is how the Web works.

The Address and Status Bars

In Internet Explorer the Address Bar is where you type, or paste, the address or URL of a Web page you want to open.

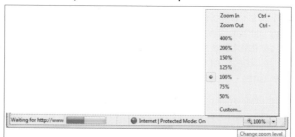

Fig. 4.3 The Address Bar

This will open the Web page shown in Fig. 4.2 when the **Go to** button → is clicked. Note that the **Go to** button then changes to the **Refresh** button ↻ which reloads the Web page shown in the **Address** bar when it is clicked.

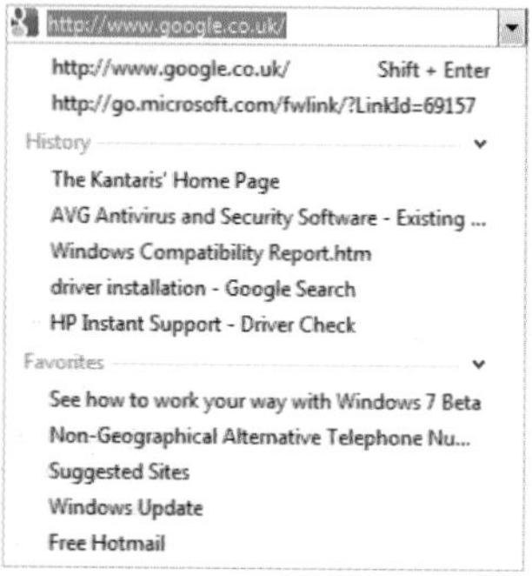

The **Address** bar is the main way of opening new Web pages when you know their URLs (Uniform Resource Locator, a fancy term for Web page address). A drop-down menu of the most recent locations you have entered, can be opened by clicking the black down-arrow at the right of the address box.

Fig. 4.4 Drop-down Menu

The **Status** bar, at the bottom of the screen (Fig. 4.5), shows the loading progress of the selected Web page. The URL of the specific Web page appears momentarily, but is then replaced by the green loading progress bar. Clicking the down-arrow at the extreme right of the **Status** bar opens a menu of zoom options, as shown in the composite screen dump below.

Fig. 4.5 The Status Bar

Explorer Buttons

As with other Windows 7 windows, **Internet Explorer** is fully equipped with toolbars, which have buttons you can left-click to quickly carry out a program function.

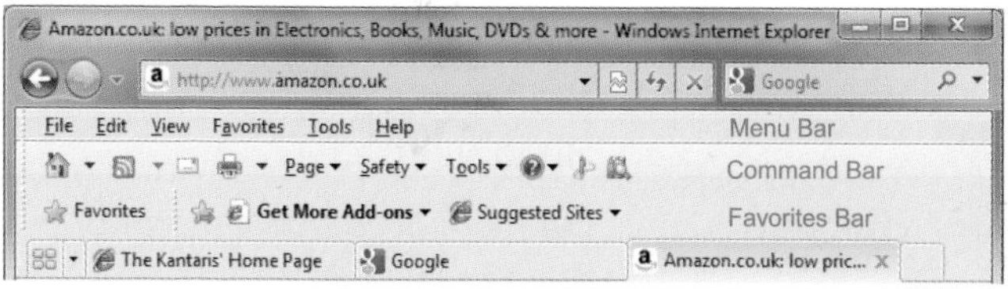

Fig. 4.6 The Internet Explorer Address Bar and Toolbars

As you can see, there are several toolbars below the Address bar, which can be switched off if you don't need them by clicking the **Tools** button on the Command Bar (below the Menu Bar) and selecting **Toolbars**, which opens the sub-menu shown in Fig. 4.7. With the **Customize**, **Add or Remove Commands** option you can control what buttons display on the Command Bar, by adding or removing them in the **Customize Toolbar** box, shown in Fig. 4.8 below. From here you can not only **Add** or **Remove** buttons, but you can also rearrange their position on the bar.

Fig. 4.7   Toolbars

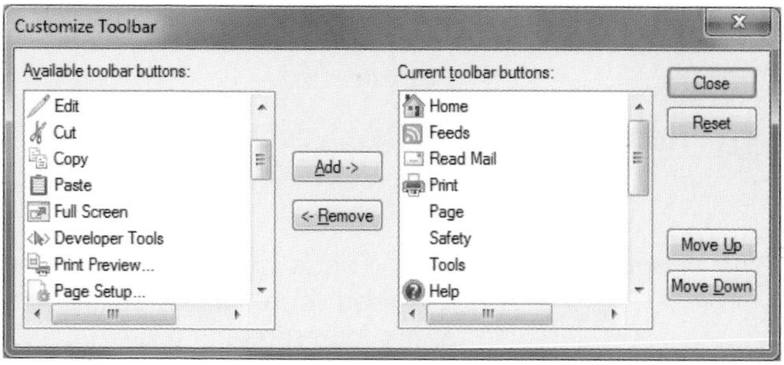

Fig. 4.8 The Customize Toolbar Box

Most of the buttons on the Address bar and other toolbars are pretty self-explanatory. Those on the Address bar have the following functions:

Button	*Function*
Back	Displays the previous page viewed. If there isn't one this is 'greyed out'.
Forward	Displays the next page on the **History** list.
Recent	Opens a drop-down menu of recent pages you have visited.
Compatibility	Improves the display of Web sites designed for older browsers.
Refresh	Brings a fresh copy of the current Web page to the viewer.
Stop	Halts any on-line transfer of page data.
Search	Searches for the text typed into the **Search** box. You can choose which search engine to use as a default by clicking the down-arrow to the right of the search box.

The Menu bar is located below the Address Bar. You can close this if you don't want it to display (see Fig. 4.7).

The Command Bar, below the Menu Bar has the following default buttons, but you can add more (see Fig. 4.8):

Button	*Function*
Home	Displays your specified home page, with a Microsoft page as the default.
Feeds	View Feeds on the open Web site. If a feed is not detected the colour of the icon remains grey.
Read Mail	Opens your mail client so that you can read your e-mail messages.

| | Print | Prints the open Web page, or frame, using the current print settings. |

| | Page ▼ | Opens a menu that allows you to open a new window, save the current page, send it or a link to it by e-mail to a recipient, zoom the page, or change the text size on it. |

| | Safety ▼ | Displays a drop-down menu that allows you to delete the browsing **History**, Browse in private, see the privacy policy of Web pages, turn on the SmartScreen Filter so that unsafe Web sites can be reported, and activate Windows Update. |

| | Tools ▼ | Displays a drop-down menu that allows you to diagnose connection problems, reopen the last browsing session, manage pop-ups, specify your Internet options, and generally control how Explorer works. |

| | **Help** | Opens a drop-down menu giving quick access to **Help** topics. |

| | **Blog This** | Opens Windows Live Writer to create or add content to your blog. |

| | **Research** | Allows you to carry out research into a specific subject. |

The Favorites Bar has the following buttons:

Button	*Function*
☆ Favorites	Opens the **Favorites Center** from which you can choose the **Favorites**, **Feeds** or **History** bars.
Add to	Adds a favourite site to the **Favorites** bar.

In addition, there are links to suggested Microsoft Web sites.

Favorites

Using Favorites, or Bookmarks, is an easy way to save Web page addresses for future use. It's much easier to select a

page from a sorted list, than to manually type a URL address into the Address field. You don't have to remember the address and are less likely to make a typing error!

With **Internet Explorer** your Favorites are kept in the **Favorites Center**, shown in Fig. 4.9, opened by clicking ⭐ Favorites, the **Favorites** button.

To keep the list open in a separate pane, you click the **Pin the Favorites Center** button 🔲. To close it again, click its **Close** button 🗵.

Fig. 4.9 Favorites Centre

Adding a Favorite – There are several ways to add a 'Favorite' to your list. When you are viewing a Web page that you want to visit again, right-click in the page and select **Add to Favorites** from the context menu. Another way is to click the **Add to Favorites** button 🔶 and select the **Add to Favorites** menu option, or you can use the **Ctrl+D** shortcut.

All of these methods open the Add a Favorite dialogue box (Fig. 4.10) in which you can give the new Favorite a name, and choose a folder to put it in. Then just click the **Add** button to finish.

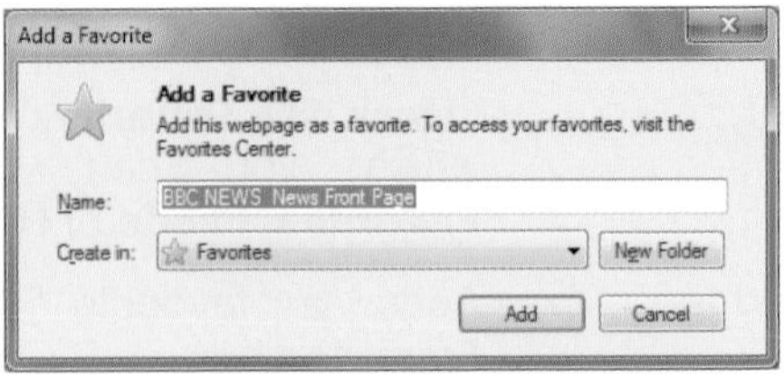

Fig. 4.10 The Add a Favorite Box

Browsing History

Internet Explorer stores details of all the Web pages and files you view on your hard disc, and places temporary pointers to them in a folder. To return to these in the future, click the **View History** tab in the **Favorites Center**, to open the **History** list shown in Fig. 4.11.

Fig. 4.11 Web Browsing History

In this list you can see what Web sites you visited in the last 3 weeks. Clicking a listed site opens links to the individual Web pages you went to. Clicking any of these will open the page again.

The length of time history items are kept on your hard disc can be set by clicking the **Tools** button and selecting **Internet Options** to open the tabbed dialogue box shown in Fig. 4.12.

Clicking the **Settings** button in the **Browsing history** section, pointed to here, opens an additional dialogue box in which you can select the number of days that **History** files are kept (between 0 and 999). To delete all history items click the **Delete** button, which will release the hard disc space used.

Fig. 4.12 General Internet Options

Web Feeds

Web feeds (feeds for short) are usually used for news and blogs and contain frequently updated content published by a Web site. You can use feeds if you want updates to a Web site to be automatically downloaded to your PC.

When you visit a Web page that contains feeds, the grey **Feeds** button on the Internet Explorer toolbar changes to orange. To look at the feeds, click the feed symbol. To get content automatically downloaded to your computer, you will need to subscribe to the feed. This is very easy to do, and doesn't cost anything! Just clicking a **Subscribe to this feed** link, like that shown in Fig. 4.13, opens the **Subscribe to this Feed** box shown in Fig. 4.14. Clicking the **Subscribe** button adds the feed to the 'Common Feed List' in the

BBC News | News Front Page | UK Edition

You are viewing a feed that contains frequently updated content. When you subscribe to a feed, it is added to the Common Feed List. Updated information from the feed is automatically downloaded to your computer and can be viewed in Internet Explorer and other programs. Learn more about feeds.

Subscribe to this feed

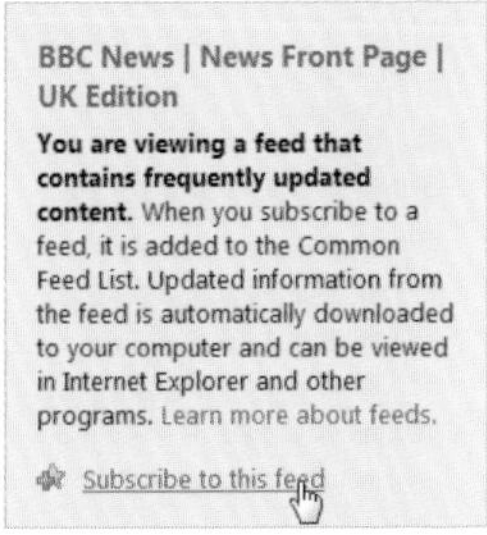

Fig. 4.13 Subscribing to a Web Feed

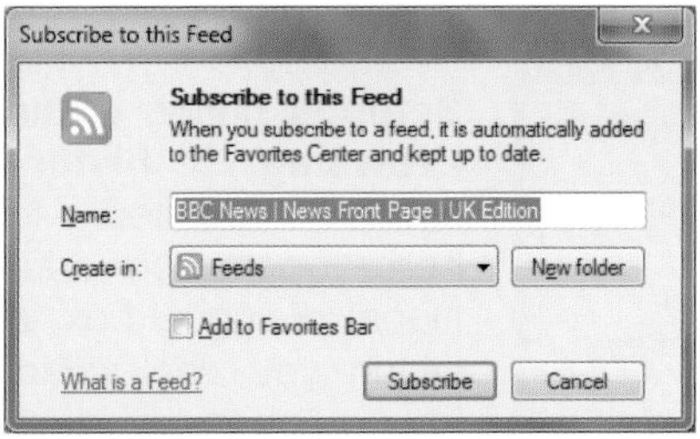

Fig. 4.14 Subscribe to this Feed Box

Favorites Center, and updated information from the feed will be automatically down-loaded to your computer for viewing in Internet Explorer.

All your subscribed feeds will be listed in the **Feeds** section of the **Favorites Center**.

Favorites | Feeds | History
Feeds for United Kingdom
Microsoft Feeds
BBC News | News Front Page | UK Edition
Telegraph Man Utd

Fig. 4.15 Feeds List

Clicking an item in the Feeds list, shown in Fig. 4.15, will open it in the main Explorer pane so you can keep up to date. We use this feature to try and keep ourselves up to date.

Tabbed Browsing

With tabbed browsing you can open several Web sites in one Explorer window each in its own tab, and switch between them by clicking on their tab. To create a new tab, click the **New Tab** icon 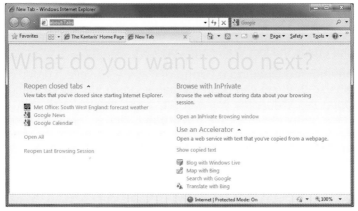, pointed to in Fig. 4.16, immediately to the right of the existing tabs.

Fig. 4.16 Creating a New Tab

The first time you do this a special tabbed browsing information page opens as shown in Fig. 4.17 below.

Fig. 4.17 The What Do you Want to Do Next Tabbed Browsing Page

Please read the above text, and note that the 'link' **about:Tabs** is highlighted in the Address Bar so you can simply type a new Web address, or click the **Favorites** button and open one of your **Favorites**.

Explorer 8 has an **InPrivate** browsing mode opened by clicking the **Browse with InPrivate** link shown above. This opens a new window with InPrivate in the Address Bar. You can then safely browse without leaving any traces. Just closing the InPrivate window returns you to standard mode.

Using Quick Tabs – When you have several Web sites open in different tabs a new button appears to the left of the first tab. This is the **Quick Tabs** button ⊞ which displays all the tabbed Web sites as thumbnail images when it is clicked, as shown in Fig. 4.18.

Fig. 4.18 Using Quick Tabs

In this view you can click a thumbnail to open its Web page, or click the **Close Tab** button ☒ on a thumbnail to close it. Clicking the **Quick Tabs** button again closes the thumbnails and opens the last Web page you were viewing.

Saving and Opening a Group of Tabs – To save a group of tabs so that you can open the pages again, do the following: Open the Web sites you want to save, maybe ones with a common theme. Click the **Favorites** button ☆ Favorites to open the Favorites Center, then click the down-arrow by the **Add to Favorites** button, and select **Add Current Tabs to Favorites** from the drop-down list.

In the displayed dialogue box give a name to the folder to contain the selected Web sites – we called it **Best Buys**, (Fig. 4.19) and click the **Add** button.

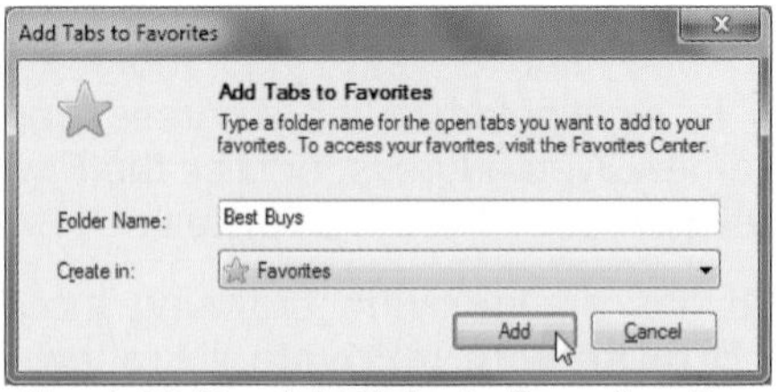

Fig. 4.19 The Add Tabs to Favorites Box

To open a group of tabs, click the **Favorites** button , select the group folder you want to open (see Fig. 4.20), and either click the arrow to the right of the folder name ➜ to open all the tabbed sites in the group, or click the folder to display all the Web sites in it and select one of them.

Fig. 4.20 Opening a Group of Tabs

Compatibility Mode

You may find that Internet Explorer 8 does not render some older Web pages correctly. One of our online banking sites for example has some problems with pagination. To resolve these types of problem, just click the **Compatibility View** button at the right end of the Address Bar. This displays the Web site as it would be if viewed in Internet Explorer 7, and usually corrects display problems like misaligned text, images, or text boxes.

This only affects the Web site that was active when you pressed the **Compatibility View** button, other sites open at the same time will still use Explorer 8 functionality.

The **Compatibility View** button only seems to appear on the Address Bar when it may be needed, so as time goes by and Web developers bring their sites up to 'scratch' you probably won't see it very often!

Internet Explorer Help

That's all we have space for on **Internet Explorer**, but don't forget the built-in **Help** system if you want to go deeper. It is accessed by pressing the **F1** function key, clicking the **Help** button 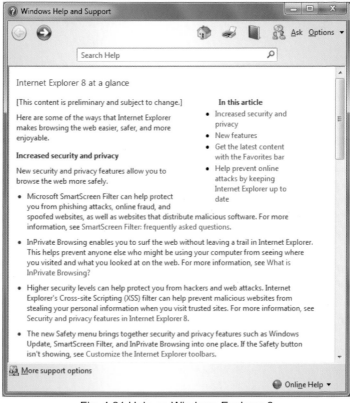 on the command bar, or clicking the **Help** Menu bar option and selecting **Internet Explorer Help** from the drop-down menu. Any of these open the screen shown in Fig. 4.21 below.

Fig. 4.21 Help on Windows Explorer 8

5

Using E-mail

 Windows 7 does not come packaged with an e-mail program, but Microsoft has made **Windows Live Essentials** available as an optional download. This includes a new version of **Windows Live Mail**, designed to work with Windows 7. Once you have downloaded and installed this, as long as you are connected to the Internet and set up correctly, you can communicate with others by e-mail. Wherever they are in the World, all you need to know is their e-mail address. In this chapter we look at Windows Live Mail, but you can use another program if you prefer.

Windows Live Essentials

Windows Live Mail is Microsoft's excellent all-in-one package for e-mail, contacts management, newsgroups, and feeds. With it you can access several different e-mail accounts from the one window, including Web based accounts from Windows Live Hotmail, MSN Hotmail, AOL, Gmail, and premium Yahoo! Accounts. Its PhotoMail feature lets you send large photographs in your messages.

You can obtain **Windows Live** from several Microsoft Web sites, including:

www.windowslive.com/Get

Have a good look around and when you are ready click the **Download now** button, select **Run** when asked, choose the components that you want (Fig. 5.1) and finally click the **Install** button to download and install them on your PC. It couldn't really be easier.

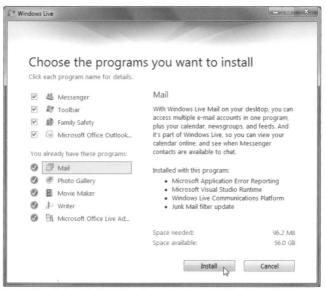

Fig. 5.1 Installing the Components of Windows Live

Windows Live Mail

To start Live Mail, click the **Start** button 🥏 open the **All Programs** menu (see page 12), click **Windows Live**, and then **Windows Live Mail**. As you will probably be using your e-mail program every time you open your PC, perhaps now would be a good time to add it to the **Taskbar**. Then in the future you just need to click its icon to get going.

Fig. 5.2
Right-click Menu

This is very easy to do, just right-click the **Windows Live Mail** entry in the **All Programs** menu and select the **Pin to Taskbar** option in the context menu, as shown here in Fig. 5.2. An icon is placed on the right of your Taskbar buttons. You can then drag it to where you want on the bar.

Connecting to your Server

When you run Live Mail for the first time, you are prompted to add an e-mail account. You will need the following information from the supplier of your e-mail service. Your e-mail address and password, the type of e-mail server to be used, and the address of the incoming and outgoing e-mail servers you should use.

If the connection process does not start automatically, use the **Tools**, **Accounts** menu command, click the **Add** button, select **E-mail Account** and click **Next** to start it manually. Follow the instructions from screen to screen. It should only take a minute. You can add all your different e-mail accounts like this and view them all from the same window.

Once your connection is established, opening the **Inbox** will display any messages waiting in your mailbox, as shown in Fig. 5.3 below.

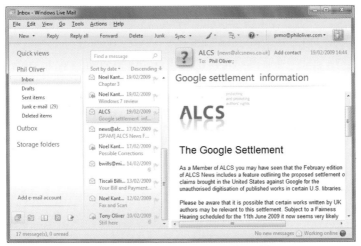

Fig. 5.3 Windows Live Mail Default View

This shows the default layout of the Windows Live Mail window, which consists of the **Folder Pane** on the left, Menu and Tool bars, a **Message List** in the centre below a **Search** box, and a **Reading Pane** on the right with a Message header above it.

The **Folder Pane** contains the active mail folders. Clicking on one of these, displays its contents in the **Message List**. Clicking on a message in the list opens a preview of it in the **Reading Pane**, while double-clicking on a message opens the message in its own window.

To check your mail at any time, click the **Sync** toolbar button ⬚ Sync which with a Broadband connection will automatically download your messages. If you are using a Dial-up connection, it will display the Dial-up Connection window, for you to connect to the Internet. Any new messages will then be downloaded from your mailbox.

A Test E-mail Message

Before explaining in more detail the main features of **Windows Live Mail** we will step through the procedure of sending a very simple e-mail message. The best way to test out any unfamiliar e-mail features is to send a test message to your own e-mail address. This saves wasting somebody else's time, and the message can be very quickly checked.

To start, click the **New** button on the toolbar ⬚ New to open the New Message window, shown in Fig. 5.4.

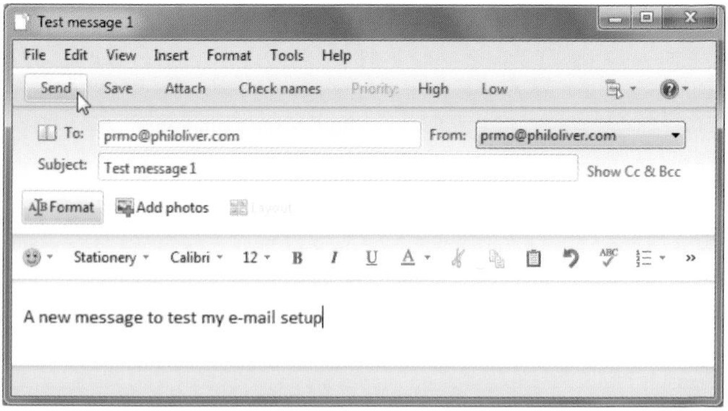

Fig. 5.4 Sending a Test Message

Type your own e-mail address in the **To:** field, and a title for the message in the **Subject:** field. The text in this subject field will form a header for the message when it is received, so it helps to show in a few words what the message is about. Next, type your message in the main body of the window and click the **Send** button ⬚Send .

By default, your message is placed in the **Outbox** folder and sent immediately if you are on Broadband, otherwise you will have to press the **Sync** button to send it.

When **Live Mail** next checks for mail, it should find the message and download it into your **Inbox** folder (Fig. 5.7).

The Main Window

Windows Live Mail uses three major windows, which we will refer to as: the Main window which opens first; the Read Message window for reading your mail; and the New Message window, to compose your outgoing mail messages.

The Main window consists of a menu, a toolbar, and three panes described next, with the default display shown in our example in Fig. 5.3. You can choose different pane layouts, and customise the toolbar, by clicking the **Menus** button ⬚▾ and choosing the **Layout**, or **Customize Toolbar** options, but we will let you try these for yourself.

The Folders List – This contains a list of your mail folders, and has shortcuts to your **Calendar** ⬚ , **Contacts** ⬚ , **Feeds** ⬚ and **Newsgroups** ⬚ , and back to **Mail** ⬚ . Each account has at least five mail folders, as shown in Fig. 5.5 on the next page. You can add your own (usually in the Storage folders section) with the **File**, **Folder**, **Create new folder** command from the Main window. You can then drag messages from the **Message List** and drop them into a folder for storage.

The **Quick views** option at the top lets you view all the unread mail you have received. This is really useful when you have multiple mail accounts open.

If you have problems with space on your screen, you can minimise the **Folders List** to a **Compact** view by dragging its right border to the left (as shown in Fig. 5.5).

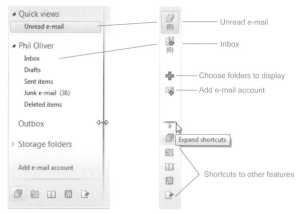

Fig. 5.5 The Default Folders List, in Normal and Compact Views

The Message List – When you select a folder, by clicking it in the **Folders List**, the **Message List** shows the contents of

that folder with brief details given for each message, as shown here in Fig. 5.6.

The first column shows a message status icon, with the most common being: unread ✉, read ✉, replied to ✉ and forwarded ✉. Next is the name of the sender and when it arrived. The second row shows the 'Subject' or title of each message followed by status icons showing, for example, if it has an attachment ✉, or has been 'flagged' ✎.

Fig. 5.6 The Message List

You can control how this pane displays by clicking the **Menus** button ✉ and choosing the **Layout**, **Message List** menu options.

To sort a list of messages, click the **Sort by ...** link and choose how you want it sorted from the drop-down menu.

To search for a message term in the list, type the term in the **Find a message** box at the top and click the ✉ button.

The Reading Pane – When you select a message in the **Message List**, by clicking it once, it is displayed in the **Reading Pane** (to the right by default), which takes up the rest of the window. This lets you read the beginning of the message without actually opening it. If it is worth reading, double-clicking the header in the **Message List**, will open the message in the Read Message window.

The Read Message Window

If you double-click a message in the **Message List** of the Main window, the Read Message window is opened as shown in Fig. 5.7 below.

Fig. 5.7 Our Test Message in the Read Message Window

This is the best window to read your mail in. It has its own menu system and self explanatory toolbar, and lets you rapidly process and move between the messages in a folder.

Windows Live Mail has an automated junk filter which scans incoming messages and automatically moves them to the junk folder if it identifies them as spam or a phishing attack. If a message gets through that you don't like, just clicking the **Junk** button ⬛ will do the same thing. You should make a habit of checking the **Junk e-mail** folder(s) every now and then, as some messages may be put there by mistake. If that happens just clicking the **Not junk** button ⬛ will move the message to your **Inbox**.

The New Message Window

Clicking the **New** button New on the Main Window toolbar opens the New Message window, shown in Fig. 5.8. This is where you create your e-mail messages in Live Mail. It is important to understand its features, so that you can get the most out of it.

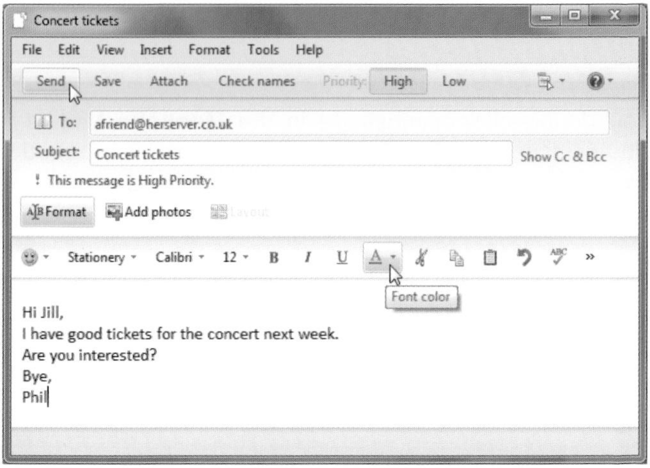

Fig. 5.8 The New Message Window

The toolbar icons in this window are all self explanatory, but if necessary, hovering the pointer over one will tell you what it does.

Message Formatting

Windows Live Mail provides quite sophisticated formatting options for an e-mail editor from both the **Format** menu and the Format toolbar. These only work if you prepare the message in HTML format, as used in Web documents. You can set this to be your default mail sending format using the Send tab in the **Tools**, **Options** box of the **Main Window**.

The **Format** toolbar shown open in Fig. 5.8 above is added to the New Message window when you are in HTML mode and all the **Format** menu options are then made active.

Photo E-mails

You can add photos to e-mail messages in two ways, as attachments (described next), or in a photo e-mail. With a photo e-mail, as long as you are signed in to Windows Live Mail with a Windows Live ID (using the e-mail address and password that you use to sign in to all Windows Live services, as described on page 75), you can upload the full versions of your photos and save them on Windows' servers. Only thumbnails of them will be placed in your message, so your e-mail will be smaller and quicker to send, but the recipient will be able to view or download the full photos.

To create a photo e-mail, click the **New** button New to open the New Message window, shown earlier in Fig. 5.4, and prepare your message as normal. Click where you want to insert photos in the message and then click the **Add photos** Add photos button. Select the photos you want to send followed by the **Add** button, and click **Done** to finish.

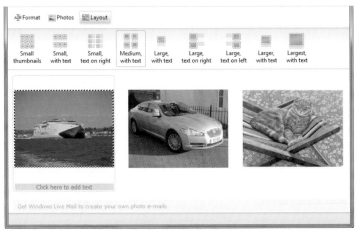

Fig. 5.9 Thumbnails in a Photo E-mail

To format your message, you click Format to format the text, Photos to add photo frames or more photos, and Layout to set the message layout, as shown in Fig. 5.9 above. Finally click the **Send** button to send your Photo e-mail. This really is well worth doing.

E-mail Attachments

To add an attachment to an e-mail message, such as a photo or work file, you simply click the **Attach** button Attach in the New Message window, select the file(s), you want to go with your message, and click **Open**.

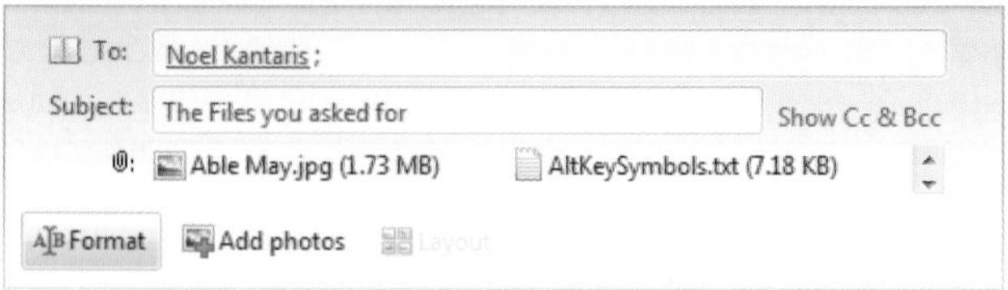

Fig. 5.10 Two Attachments Ready to Send

In **Windows Live Mail** the attached files are placed below the **Subject** box. In Fig. 5.10 we show two attachments with their icons telling the recipient what each file is; a graphics (**.jpg**) file and a Notepad (**.txt**) text file in our case. Finally click the **Send** button to send your e-mail.

Receiving Attachments

Fig. 5.11, on the facing page, shows an e-mail we received with three attachments in a Read Message window.

The received message shows the graphics (**.jpg**) file open at the bottom of the window, and all three attachments in the Header bar with icons indicating what type of files they are.

Right-clicking an attachment opens a drop-down menu as shown in Fig. 5.11. From this you can choose to open, print or save the attached files. The **Save all** option is the one most often used.

Double-clicking an attached file icon opens a Mail Attachment window showing you the type of document and asking whether you want to open it. A graphics file (**.jpg**) then opens in **Windows Live Photo Gallery**, and a Word document file opens in Microsoft Word.

As long as you have the necessary programs, each attached file can be opened in situ or saved to disc from within the application that opened it.

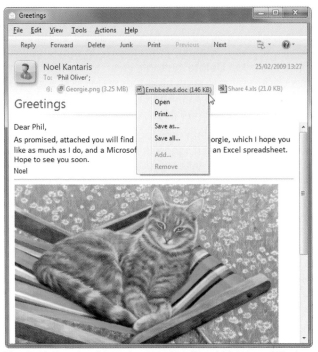

Fig. 5.11 Received Attachments in a Read Message Window

Replying to a Message

When you receive an e-mail message that you want to reply to, Live Mail makes it very easy to do.

With the message you want to reply to open, click the **Reply** button [Reply] to open the New Message window. The reply address and the subject field are both filled automatically for you, and the text of the message you are replying to will, by default, be placed under the insertion point.

You can edit this text, so that it is obvious what you are referring to. Just a few lines may well be enough. Then type your reply, format whatever you want and click the **Send** button [Send].

Deleting Messages

Some e-mail messages you receive will be worth keeping, but most will need deleting. From the Read Message window you just click the **Delete** button  to do this. From the Main window you can select the messages you don't want to keep in the **Messages Lis**t and either, click the **Delete** button , or press the **Delete** key.

Whenever you delete a message it is actually moved to the **Deleted Items** folder. If ignored, this folder gets bigger and bigger over time, so you need to check it frequently and manually re-delete messages you will not need again.

To get this done automatically, you use the **Tools**, **Options** menu command to open the Options dialogue box, click the Advanced tab and click the **Maintenance** button at the bottom of the screen and check the **Empty messages from the 'Deleted Items' folder on exit** box in the displayed Maintenance screen. Your deletions will then be fully removed whenever you close Windows Live Mail.

Spell Checking Messages

Just because e-mail messages are a quick way of getting in touch with friends and family, there is no reason why they should be full of spelling mistakes, as Windows Live Mail has a good spelling checker built in.

To try it out, prepare a message in the New Message window, but with obvious spelling mistakes, maybe like ours. Errors will be underlined in red, as shown in Fig. 5.12.

Fig. 5.12 Correcting
Spelling Mistakes

Right-clicking a flagged 'error' opens a drop-down menu. You can accept one of the suggestions, **Ignore All** occurrences in the message, or add your original word to the dictionary for future use. This works very well.

Printing Messages

Windows Live Mail lets you print e-mail messages to paper, but it doesn't give you any control over the page settings it uses. When you are ready to print a message, if it is open in the Read Message window, click the **Print** button [Print]. In the **Message List** use the **Ctrl+P** key combination, or the **File**, **Print** menu command. All of these open the standard Windows Print dialogue box which allows you to select one of your printers, the **Page Range**, and **Number of copies** you want. Clicking the **Print** button will start the process.

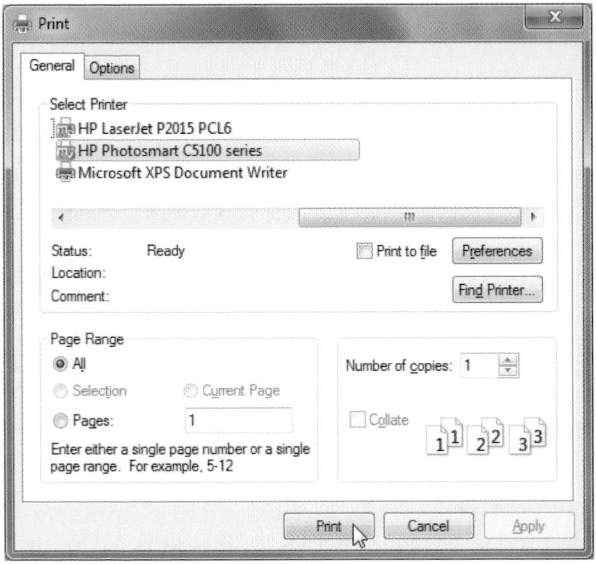

Fig. 5.13 The Windows Print Dialogue Box

The Contacts Folder

Windows Live Mail lets you create and keep a contact list to store details such as the names, addresses, phone numbers, and e-mail addresses of your contacts, or people you communicate with most.

If you have never signed in to Live Mail with a Windows Live ID (page 75), your contact list will contain only the contacts you have added or imported into the program. If you are signed in, Live Mail uses the contact list associated with your Windows Live ID and any changes that you make to your contacts in Live Mail will be saved and also used in Windows Live Messenger, Windows Live Hotmail, and other Windows Live products and services.

In Live Mail you click the **Contacts** button 📖 at the bottom of the **Folder Pane** to access the **Contacts** window.

Fig. 5.14 The Live Mail Contacts Window

Here in Fig. 5.14 we show a small part of a **Contacts** folder. You can add a person's details in the **Add a Contact** box opened by clicking the **New** button New , as shown in Fig. 5.15 on the facing page.

Use the Contact tab to enter the name, phone, and e-mail details for your new contact. The Personal tab screen is used to enter their personal address, phone and fax numbers, and Web site. You can also enter similar information for Work.

The rest of the information can be entered if you have the time, or be entered later by editing the Contact's entry.

Unfortunately, there does not seem to be any facility for adding photos of your contacts, as in earlier versions.

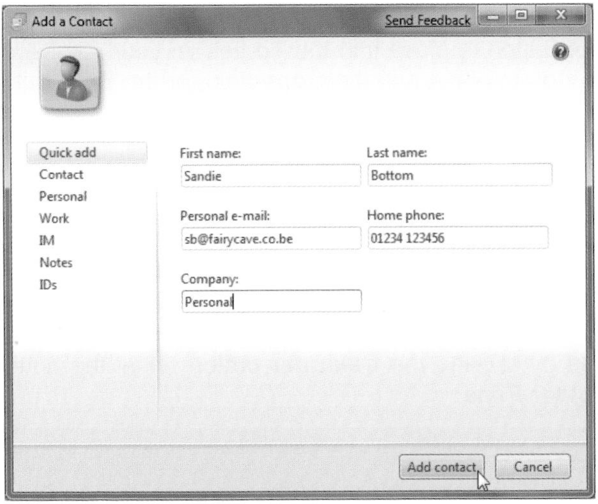

Fig. 5.15 The Add a Contact Window

To send a new message from your **Contacts** list, highlight their name and click the **E-mail** button E-mail to open a pre-addressed New Message window in Live Mail.

Or, from the New Message window, start typing a name in the ⊞ To: box and select from the options presented, or click on the ⊞ To: button, or use the **Tools**, **Select from contacts** command, to open the **Send an E-mail** box.

Fig. 5.16
Selecting a Contact

In this box, you can select a person's name and click either the **To:** button to place it in the **To** field of your message, the **Cc:** button to place it in the **Copy** field, or the **Bcc:** button to place it in the **Blind Copy** field (so that the address will not be visible to the main recipient of the message).

The Windows Calendar

Windows Live Mail also provides you with a calendar which is opened by clicking the **Calendar** button 📅 at the bottom of the **Folder Pane**.

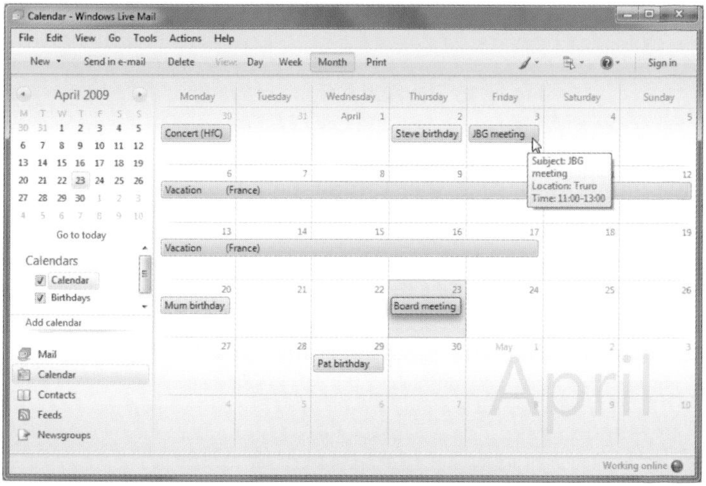

Fig. 5.17 The Live Mail Calendar

This will provide you with all the scheduling tools you should ever need. It provides day, week and month views, and supports multiple, colour-coded calendars, making it easy to keep schedules for work, family, school and hobbies, etc.

We will leave it to you to explore this excellent facility on your own.

Getting Help

As you would expect, Live Mail has a **Help** system if you want to go deeper. It is opened in an Internet Explorer window by clicking the **Help** button 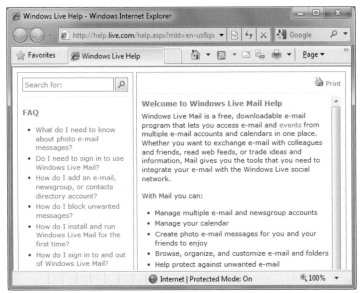, pressing the **F1** function key, or clicking the **Help** Menu bar option and selecting **Get Help with Mail** from the drop-down menu. All of these open the screen shown in Fig. 5.18 below.

Fig. 5.18 Help with Windows Live Mail

Windows Live ID

You don't have to sign in with a Windows Live ID to use Windows Live Mail, but if you do, you can connect to other Windows Live services and use extra features of Live Mail. When you are signed in, Live Mail uses the contact list and calendars associated with your Windows Live ID and keeps them synchronised for you automatically.

To sign in to Windows Live ID from Live Mail, click the **Sign in** button `Sign in` in the upper-right corner of the Live Mail Main window (see Fig. 5.17).

Sign in - Windows Live ID

Sign in to Windows Live Mail and do more

- Use the same contact list as on the Windows Live website.
- See when senders are online in Messenger.
- Sync with your Windows Live Calendar on the web.

About signing in

One Windows Live ID gets you into Hotmail, Messenger, Xbox Live—and all Windows Live ID sites and services.
Don't have a Windows Live ID?

Windows Live ID (example555@hotmail.com)

Password

☑ Remember my password   Forgot your password?

Sign in   Cancel

Fig. 5.19 Signing in to Windows Live ID

If you have them, type your Windows Live ID and password, into the boxes shown above and click **Sign in**. If not, click the **Don't have a Windows Live ID?** link, and then follow the on-screen instructions to sign up. It really doesn't take very long to get one.

If you tick the **Remember my password** check box, you won't have to remember it again in the future. But of course, you should only do this on your own personal computer.

Once you have signed in the procedure is automatic whenever you open Windows Live Mail. To sign out again, use the **Tools**, **Options** menu command and click the **Stop signing in** button on the Connection tab sheet shown in Fig. 5.20 below.

Connecting to Windows Live services

Signing in with a Windows Live ID connects Mail to other Windows Live services like Contacts, Messenger, and Spaces.

Sign in with another ID   Stop signing in

Fig. 5.20 Signing out of Windows Live ID

6

Looking After Your PC

Windows 7 comes equipped with a full range of utilities for you to easily maintain your PC's health and wellbeing. You can access most of these tools by selecting **System Tools** from the **Start**, **All Programs**, **Accessories** menu, which opens the group of options shown here in Fig. 6.1.

Fig. 6.1 System Tools

Quite an impressive list, but of all the available tools, **System Information** is the easiest to take a first look at – it displays such things as your Operating System, System Summary, Hardware Resources, etc. As each one of these is bound to be different for different PCs, we leave it to you to examine the information for your own system.

Problem Prevention

Windows 7 has strong protection against System corruption:

- System Protection
- Automatic Update
- System Restore

These will be discussed shortly, but now might be a good time to copy your data to a DVD or external hard drive, as discussed in Chapter 3. After all, hard discs do 'crash' and your PC could be stolen, or lost in a fire, or flood. Any of these events would cause a serious data loss, so it's a good idea to have copies stored away safely.

System Protection

Windows applications sometimes can, and do, overwrite important **System** files. However, Windows tends to protect your **System** files by automatically restoring them to their original version, if any changes have been attempted by an application program.

Automatic Update

Windows can automatically update any **System** files as they become available from Microsoft's Web site. To make sure this happens, click **Start, All Programs**, and select the **Windows Update** menu option, shown here in Fig. 6.2, and you will be connected to Microsoft's Web site.

Click the **Check for updates** link on the left panel in Fig. 6.3, to get a list of updates for your system. If critical updates are available, these are automatically installed, provided this option was selected (see **Change settings** below). Non-critical updates can be viewed before selecting the ones you might want to install. There is no point downloading updates that have no relevance to you!

Fig. 6.2 Windows Update

The **Change settings** link (second on the list of links on the left panel) displays a window in which you can choose to **Install updates automatically**, as recommended by Microsoft. This should guarantee you are always up to date, which is important to make sure that as possible security issues are found and corrected by Microsoft they are installed on your system straight away.

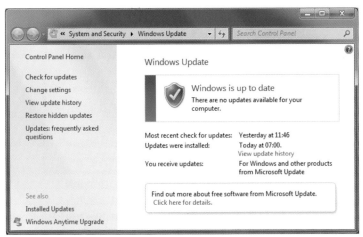

Fig. 6.3 Checking for Windows Updates

System Restore

 System Restore automatically backs up registry and system files whenever you install new software or drivers, and enables you to restore your computer to an earlier state without losing any of your data files (such as e-mail messages, documents, or photos). You would typically use System Restore if your computer starts misbehaving after an update or a new software installation. Restoring your PC to an earlier restore point may well resolve the problem. Do note, however, that software (programs) installed since the restore point was made will be removed from your PC, but not data.

Every time you start to install a new program, System Restore takes a snapshot of your system prior to starting the new installation.

To examine the utility, click the **Start** button, type **restore** in the search field, and select System Restore from the resulting list. You can also use the **Start, All Programs, Accessories, System Tools** menu command and select **System Restore**. Both methods open the first (explanatory) screen of a three-screen **System Restore** utility, as shown in Fig. 6.4 on the next page.

Fig. 6.4 The System Restore Opening Window

Clicking the **Next** button opens the second **System Restore** screen shown in Fig. 6.5 below.

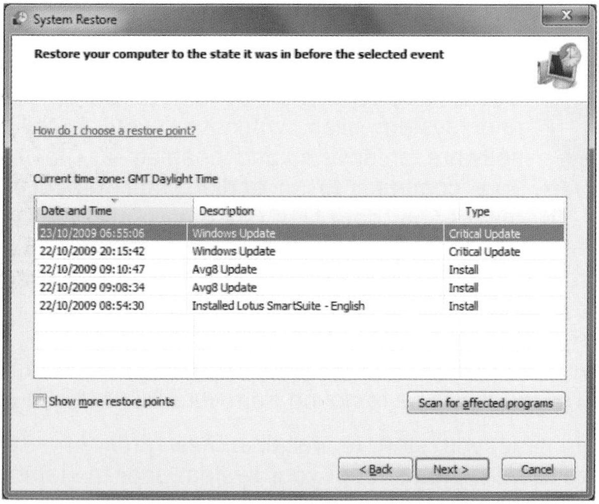

Fig. 6.5 A Recently Available System Restore Point

You may well have more than five System Restore Points when you try this. Selecting a restore point from the list and clicking **Next** opens the final **System Restore** screen. Once you confirm that this is what you want to do, the restore process starts. Until this process finishes, you should not switch off your computer, or you might end up in real trouble.

To create a new restore point, click the **Start** button ⊕, type **create restore point** in the search field, and select ⊡ Create a restore point from the resulting list. This opens the multi-tab **System Properties** dialogue box, shown in Fig. 6.6 below, with the **System Protection** tab selected.

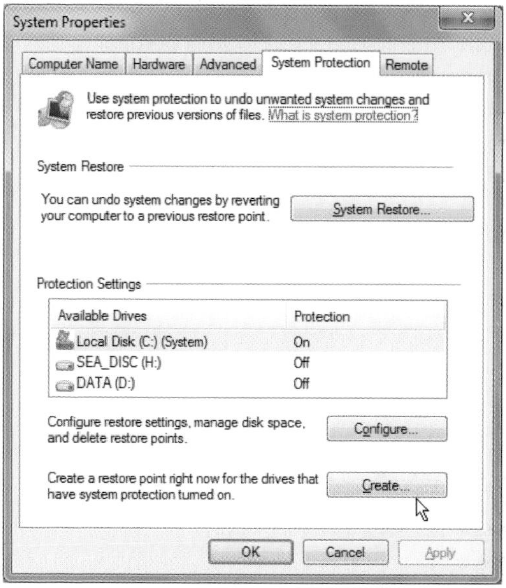

Fig. 6.6 Setting a New System Restore Point

Our two external hard drives above only contain data, not system files, so were not selected by the system. To create a **System Restore Point**, click the **Create** button which displays the box shown in Fig. 6.7.

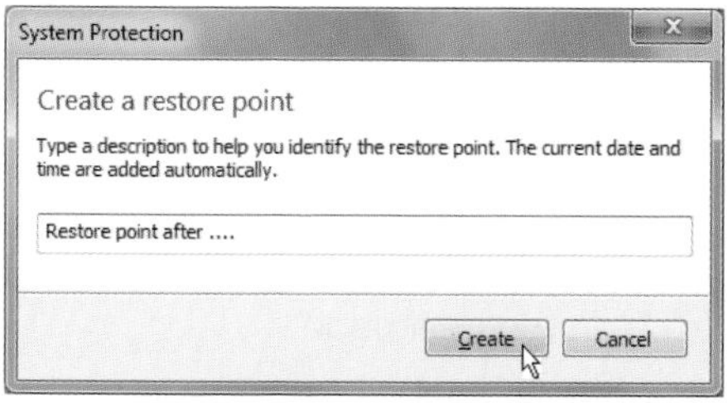

Next, type a suitable description to identify your restore point, and

Fig. 6.7 Creating a Restore Point

click the **Create** button. Windows will notify you of the success or otherwise of the operation.

The System and Security Centre

 To examine the options available in the Windows **System and Security** centre, click the **Start** button, **Control Panel**, choose to **View by: Category**, and click the **System and Security** icon, shown here, to display the window in Fig. 6.8 below.

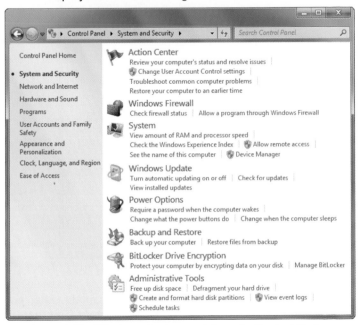

Fig. 6.8 The Windows System and Security Centre Window

For your PC to be secure, make sure that the Windows Firewall is switched on. Clicking the **Check firewall status** link, displays the screen shown in Fig. 6.9 on the next page.

A **Firewall** is a software security system that sits between your computer and the outside world and is used to set restrictions on what information is passed to and from the Internet. In other words it protects you from uninvited access.

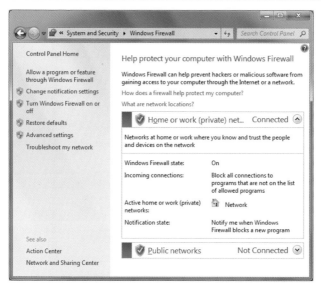

Fig. 6.9 The Windows Security Centre Window

If your firewall is turned off, or you do not have up-to-date virus protection, the **System and Security** centre will flag an error by placing the icon in the notification area of the Taskbar.

Disk Cleanup

Disk Cleanup locates and removes unnecessary files on your computer and frees up space on your hard drive(s). To start it, click the **Start** button , type **cleanup** in the search field, and click Disk Cleanup. Select the drive you want to clean up, as in Fig. 6.10 and **Disk Cleanup** then scans the drive, and lists temporary files, Internet cache files, and other files that you can safely delete, as shown in Fig. 6.11 on the next page.

Fig. 6.10 Selecting the Drive

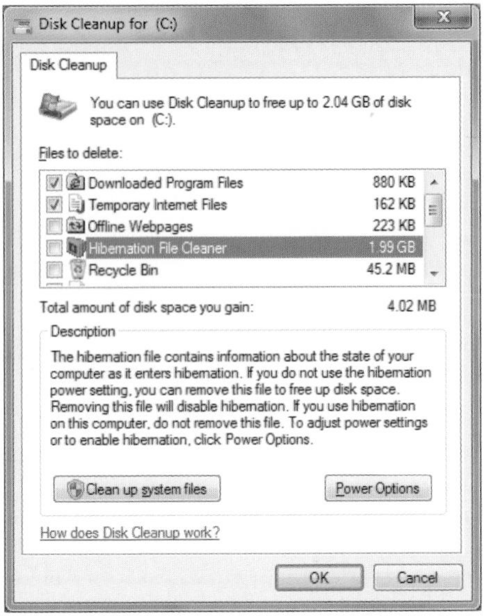

Fig. 6.11 Files Found that can be Cleaned Up

As you can see, on our setup, we could free some disc space by deleting all the files selected (the longer you use your PC the larger the files that could be deleted), and even more by deleting the **Hibernation File Cleaner** as well.

Please do not proceed with the latter deletion, though, until you highlight its entry and read the displayed small print (see Fig. 6.11 above), or you may have some regrets later, especially if you are using a Laptop.

If you delete the Hibernation Files, by ticking the check box alongside the **Hibernation File Cleaner** entry, your PC will lose the ability to **Hibernate**, and getting it back can be a bit complicated.

If you don't use hibernation there is no problem. Clicking the **OK** button, starts the cleaning process and removes all the 'unnecessary' files you selected.

Defragmenting your Hard Discs

The **Disk Defragmenter** optimises your hard discs by rearranging their data to eliminate unused spaces, which speeds up access by all of Windows operations. By default **Disk Defragmenter** is set to run automatically in Windows 7, but you can also analyse and defragment your discs and drives manually. These days you don't even need to close running applications before starting **Disk Defragmenter**.

To start the process, click the **Start** button 🔵, type **defrag** in the search field, and select 📄 Disk Defragmenter from the resulting list. Select the disc you want to defragment, and click the **Analyze disk** button to see if the disc needs to be defragmented.

If the percentage of fragmentation on the disc is high, you should click the **Defragment disk** button and start the process. You can defragment a drive in the background by minimising the window to the **Taskbar** and carry on with your work as normal.

Backing up your Data

Anyone can lose files by: accidentally deleting or replacing them, a virus attack, a software or hardware failure, such as a complete hard disc failure. With Windows, you can use **System Restore** to recover your system files, you can reinstall your programs, but what about your precious data files? To protect these, you should regularly create backups, or sets of copies of your data files, stored in a different location.

Too many people don't think about backing up their data until it has already been lost! Please don't let this happen to you. Windows 7 makes backing up easy, and has a range of features to seamlessly protect your data.

Windows 7 allows you to either back up your data files or make a complete PC backup of your entire computer.

The Backup and Restore Center

This is where you carry out your PC backup. However, before you start, it should be obvious that making a complete PC backup requires you to have some sort of an external hard drive, one that plugs into a USB port, but is at least the same size as the internal drive. This can cost less than £60, but believe us it is worth it. If you have one, plug it in now.

You can open the **Backup and Restore** center from the **Control Panel** but it is easier to click the **Start** button, type **backup** in the search field, and select [Backup and Restore] from the resulting list. This opens the window shown in Fig. 6.12.

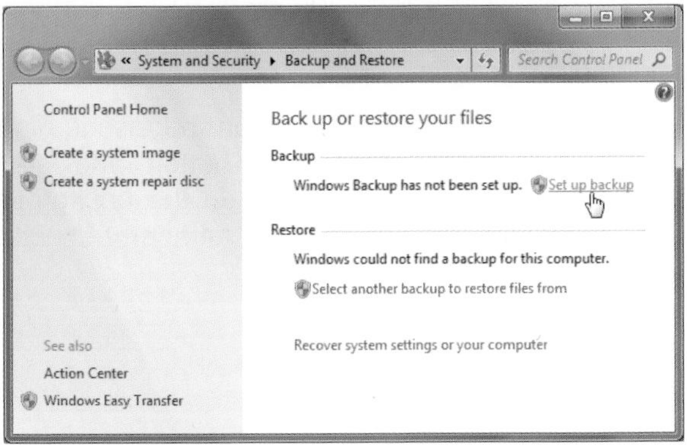

Fig. 6.12 The Backup and Restore Center

As you can see, the first time you initiate this procedure, you are required to configure **backup**, by clicking the **Set up**

Fig. 6.13 Configuring Backup

backup link pointed to above. This opens the window shown in Fig. 6.13 asking you to wait while Windows has a look at your system to see whether you have a suitable drive on which to make the backup.

The Set up backup window, shown in Fig. 6.14 below, opens next in which you are prompted to select the location to save your backup.

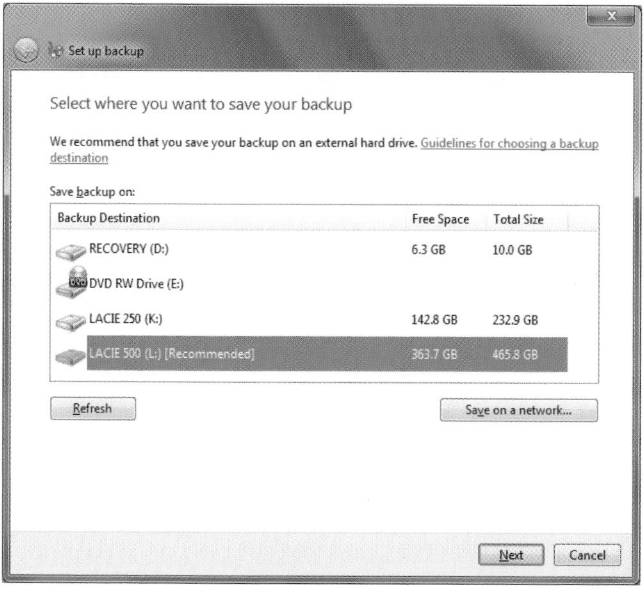

Fig. 6.14 Selecting Where to Save Your Backup

In this case, the L: drive, recommended for the backup, was one of two external USB drives. In this computer drive D: was a partition on the C: drive which holds all the system recovery data files. All of our data folders and files are in folders and Libraries on the C: drive itself. Yours is probably very much the same.

Make your selection and click the **Next** button which opens the window shown in Fig. 6.15 on the next page. Here you are asked to decide what you want to do. The recommended choice will make a complete backup of your PC, while the second choice allows you to specify what you want to back up and whether to include an image of your system or not.

We were using the Ultimate version of Windows 7, and the option of creating a system image might not be available in all versions of the program.

Fig. 6.15 Choosing an Option for the Backup

Selecting the second choice (**Let me choose**), displays the window in Fig. 6.16 below in which we have selected all our Libraries, some additional data folders in the folders tree, but not to **Include a system image of drive C:**.

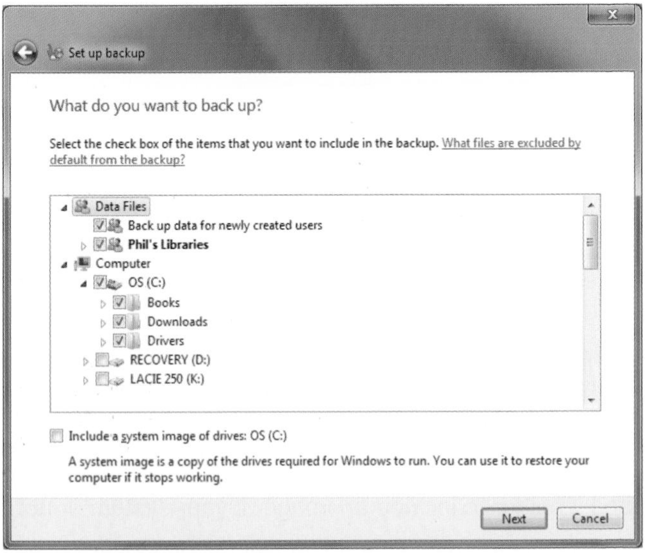

Fig. 6.16 Selecting What to Include in the Backup

The next window (Fig. 6.17) gives a summary of what you have chosen to back up and when future backups will be made. If you click the **Change schedule** link, you can set how often you want backups to be automatically carried out, these can be daily, weekly or monthly. The first time you do this, Windows carries out a full backup of your data files, later scheduled backups will only include new, or modified, files. Choose the settings you want and click the **Save settings and run backup** button.

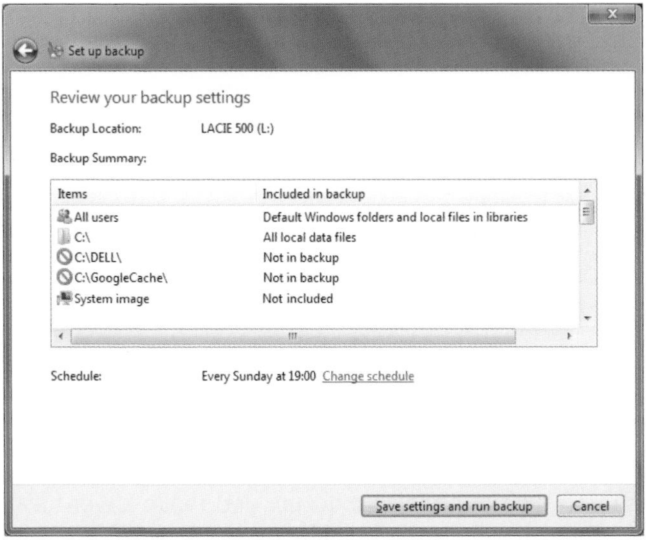

Fig. 6.17 Setting the Schedule for Creating Backups

The backup process then starts, as shown in Fig. 6.18 on the next page. This can take some time, depending on your system and on how much data is being backed up. Our first full backup took several hours, but subsequent ones usually take a lot less time. This is no problem though, as you can carry on working during the process.

To see how the backup process is going, click the **View Details** button. This opens an additional window with a progress bar and a **Stop backup** button you can click to end the process at any time.

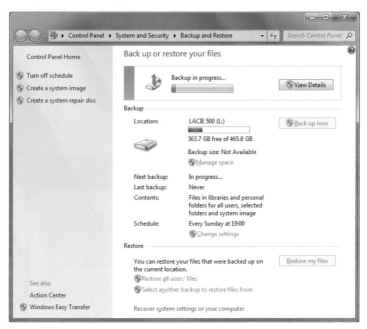

Fig. 6.18 The Backup and Restore Control Panel

Subsequent Backups

Once you create the initial backup, you really never have to think about backing up your files again since Windows will regularly do this for you according to the schedule you set.

 When you create a backup, a special backup folder is placed on the destination drive. Double-clicking its icon (shown here), opens the window shown in Fig. 6.19. From here you can restore your files, or manage the space used by your backups. You can, for instance, delete older backups to save disc space.

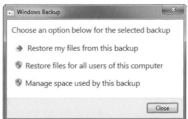

Fig. 6.19 Configuring Backup

Restoring from Backups

Restoring files and folders from your backups is very easy. You do it from the **Backup and Restore** center (see page 86), shown in Fig. 6.20 below.

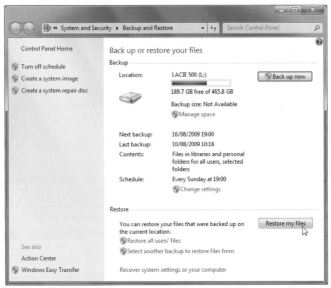

Fig. 6.20 The Backup and Restore Center

Clicking the **Restore my files** button, starts the procedure for restoring specific files and folders from the last backup.

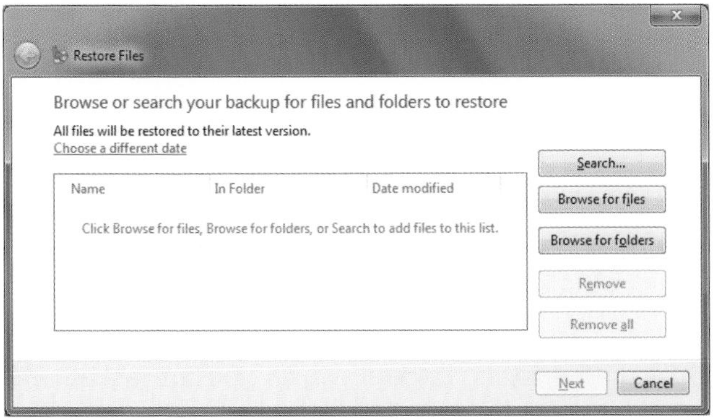

Fig. 6.21 The Restore Files Screen

You can select whether you want to restore files from the latest or an older backup, browse for files or folders, or search for a specific file or folder, before clicking the **Next** button to continue.

Fig. 6.22 Selecting a Data File to Restore

Select the files or folders you want to restore, then click the **Add files** button to display the window in Fig. 6.23.

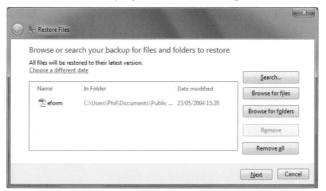

Fig. 6.23 The Selected Files to be Restored

Clicking the **Next** button, opens the window shown in Fig. 6.24 on the facing page in which you are asked where you want to restore the selected file(s).

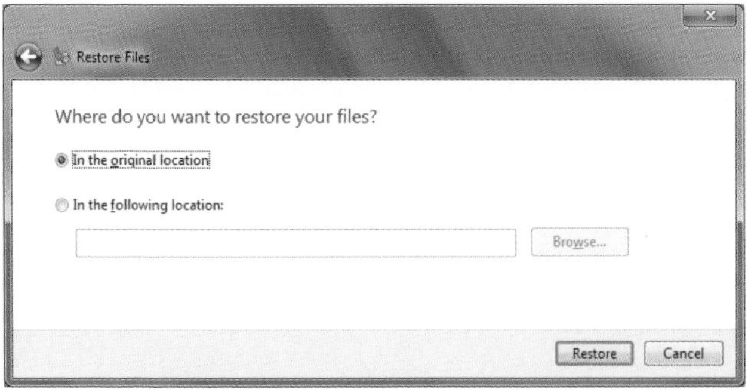

Fig. 6.24 Specifying the Restore Location

You would normally pick to restore your selection to their original location, unless you want them somewhere else of course. Finally click the **Restore** button which displays the window in Fig. 6.25.

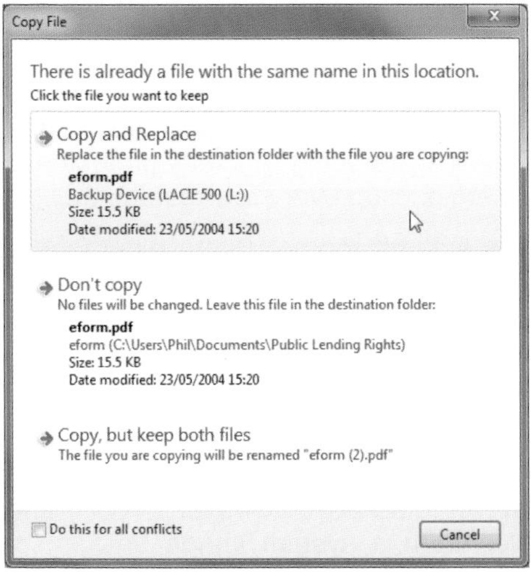

Fig. 6.25 The Copy File Window

To restore everything from the latest backup, start the **Backup and restore** center, click the **Restore my files** button (see Fig. 6.20), then click the **Browse for folders** button (see Fig. 6.21) and finally click the actual backup folder on the left on the screen of Fig. 6.26 and select in turn each sub-folder (in our case Backup of C: and Backup of K:) and press the **Add folder** button after each selection. In this way all the files on drives C: and K: will be restored

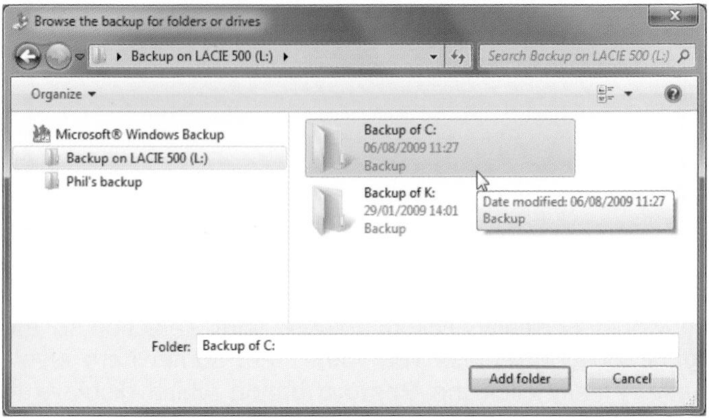

Fig. 6.26 Restoring Everything from a Backup

We are very impressed with Windows 7's backup and restore facilities. They are easy to use, and once you have set a procedure in motion you can forget it, safe in the knowledge that your data files are being regularly protected. Don't forget to do a complete backup every few months though!

If you have enough room on your external storage drive, backing up an image of your PC's drive (by either selecting the **Include a system image** option in Fig. 6.16, or using the **Create a system image** option in the **Backup and Restore** center), is a good idea.

A system image is a copy of the drive required for Windows to run, and can be used to restore your computer if the hard drive crashes. However, you cannot restore individual files from a system image backup, only the full image.

7

Controlling Your PC

The main way to control your PC is from the **Control Panel**, which provides quick and easy ways to change the hardware and software settings of your system.

Fig. 7.1 Opening the Control Panel

To access the **Control Panel**, click the **Start** button 🌐, then left-click the **Control Panel** button on the Start menu, pointed to here in Fig. 7.1.

This opens the Control Panel window in the default **Category** view, shown in Fig. 7.2 on the next page.

From here, you can add new hardware, remove or change programs, change the display type and its resolution, change the printer fonts, change your region and time settings, control your computer's setup and security, change size of the screen font, and change the keyboard repeat rate, etc.

In other words, once you know your way round the Control Panel, you can set up Windows 7 just how you want it.

Fig. 7.2 The Windows 7 Control Panel in Category View

Each option, shown above, has a listing below it relevant to that category. Also, note there is the usual **Search** box at the top-right of the window. In Fig. 7.3 we typed **sight** in the **Search** box and what we needed immediately appeared below. This is cool.

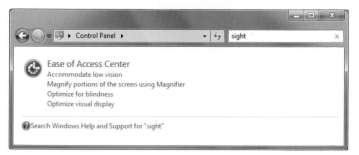

Fig. 7.3 Control Panel Search Results

However daunting it may look, it is a very good idea to get familiar with the **Control Panel** features. You may find this easier from the **Large Icons** view, shown in Fig. 7.4 on the next page, which is opened from the **View by** drop-down menu shown open at the top of Fig. 7.2.

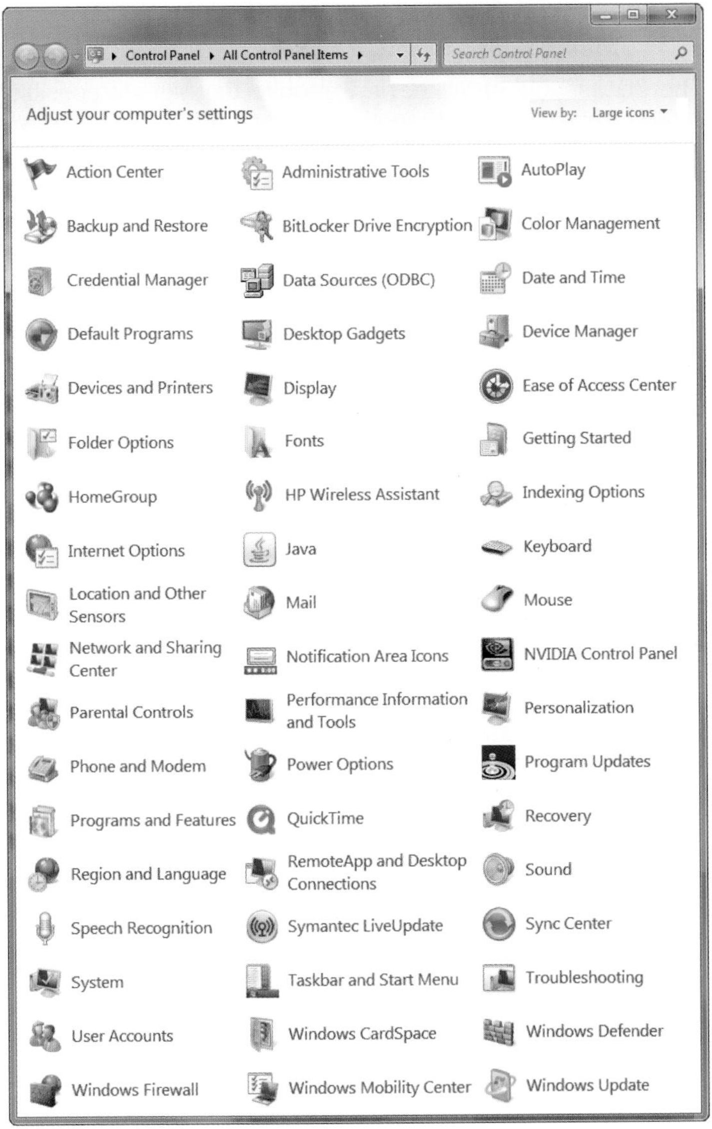

Fig. 7.4 The Control Panel in Large Icons View

The actual options available in your **Control Panel** depend on your PC hardware, and your version of Windows 7.

Changing your Display

The 3D aspects of Windows 7 require the highest possible screen resolution that your graphics card is capable of delivering. Higher screen resolution gives you better text clarity, sharper images, and more items fit on your screen, in other words you can see more. At lower resolutions, less items fit on the screen, and images may appear with jagged edges.

For example, a display resolution of 800 × 600 pixels (picture elements) is low, while one of 1600 × 1200 pixels is high. In general, LCD monitors can support higher resolutions than CRT monitors and whether you can increase your screen resolution depends on the size and capability of your monitor and the type of video card installed in your computer.

To find out if you can increase the display resolution of your computer screen, try the following:

In the **Control Panel** window (Fig. 7.2), click the **Adjust screen resolution** link, in the **Appearance and Personalization** section to open the Display Settings box shown in Fig. 7.5 below.

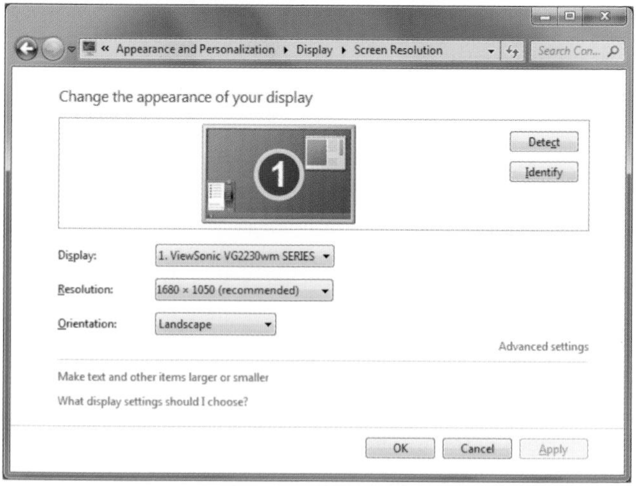

Fig. 7.5 The Display Settings Box

In this box, you can click the **Identify** button to find out the type of display your PC is using or whether an external monitor is connected to your computer. You can also change the **Resolution** and **Orientation** of your screen and make text and icons larger. For these new settings to take effect, click the **Apply** button, but before the new settings are set, you'll be asked to log off, so make sure any work you were doing has been saved! For full details on this press the **F1** key to open the **Help** window on **Getting the best display on your monitor**.

Next, try clicking the **Change the theme** link in the **Appearance and Personalization** section of the **Control Panel**, to open the window in Fig. 7.6.

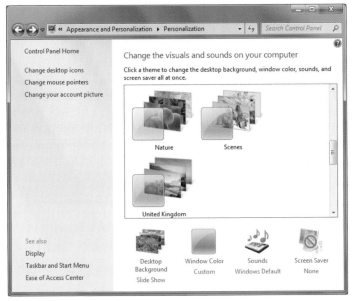

Fig. 7.6 Windows 7 Theme Options

Plenty to explore here. For example, you can change the **Desktop Background** (Fig. 7.7), control the **Window Color**, set the **Sounds** the system makes, or set a **Screen Saver**.

With Windows 7 you can choose multiple background images which cycle through a slide show, as shown in

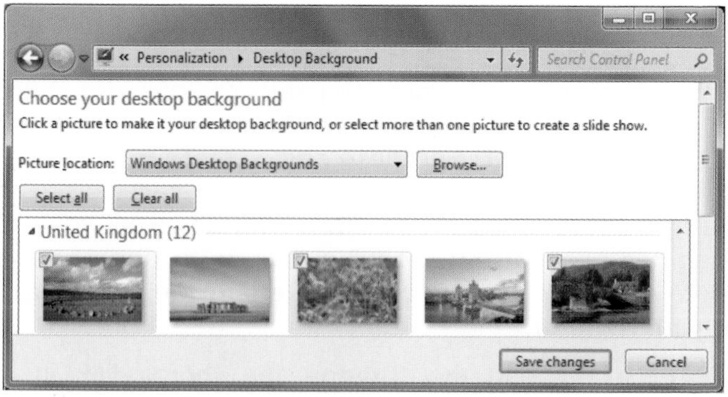

Fig. 7.7 Creating a Slide Show Background

Fig. 7.7 above. You can choose from the **Windows Desktop Backgrounds**, or click **Browse** and select your own photos. Bear in mind that the simpler your screen background the easier it is to see your desktop icons, if you use them. Well worth a good play here.

Clicking the **Window Color** link opens the window in Fig. 7.8 below. If the transparency of the open windows on your desktop is getting on your nerves, just uncheck **Enable transparency**. We also find that the **Color intensity** is best set fairly high on the slider otherwise it is sometimes difficult to see which item in a window is selected.

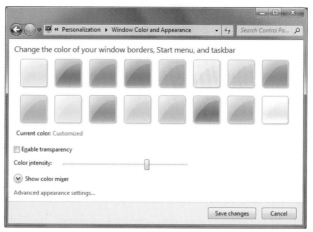

Fig. 7.8 Changing the Colour and Appearance of Windows

Clicking the **Screen Saver** link in Fig. 7.6 opens the window shown in Fig. 7.9 below.

Fig. 7.9 Selecting a Screen Saver

Clicking the down-arrow on the **Screen saver** box reveals a drop-down menu of screen savers you can choose from. We quite like the **Bubbles** one, which doesn't clear the screen, but drifts a cloud of transparent bubbles over it. Very classy.

On this window you can also change the time of inactivity before the screen saver starts up. With some, clicking the **Settings** button displays a box for you to control the screen saver display settings.

When you make all the changes you want, click the **Preview** button to see the effect of the selected options in full screen. When you are happy, stop the preview, then click the **Apply** button followed by the **OK** button. But don't then spend hours watching your screen saver, unless you've nothing else to do, of course!

Controlling Devices and Printers

When your computer was first set up, your devices and printers should have been installed automatically. If not, select **View devices and printers** in the **Hardware and Sound** section of the **Control Panel**, or click the **Start** button and choose **Devices and Printers** from the right column of the **Start** menu. Both of these open the **Devices and Printers** window, shown in Fig. 7.10 below.

Fig. 7.10 The Devices and Printers Folder

Our **Devices and Printers** folder displays six devices and seven printers and faxes as shown above. In the case of the printers, two are physical ones for printing to paper and three for creating formatted print documents **(.pdf** and **.xps)**.

With Windows 7, most devices and printers are automatically detected at installation time, or during the boot-up process, called **Plug and Play**. So if you add a new printer or a new device, like a camera, to your system it should be recognised. You may be asked for the necessary driver files if they are not already in the Windows directory, but these come on a CD, or can be found on the manufacturer's Web site.

Configuring your Printer

To control your printer, double-click its icon in the **Devices and Printers** folder (Fig. 7.10), to open a Printer Control window like that shown in Fig. 7.11 below.

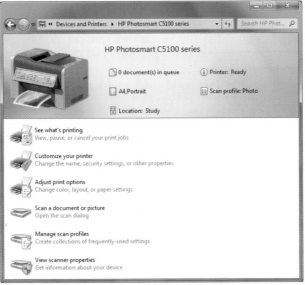

Fig. 7.11 The Printer Control Window

Here you can control what is waiting to be printed, customise your printer, and set all the printer's parameters, such as the printer port (or network path), paper and graphics options, built-in fonts, and other device options specific to the printer.

A newly installed printer is automatically set as the default printer, indicated by a green tick against ✅ it in the **Devices and Printers** folder. To change the default printer, select a printer connected to your PC, right-click it, and choose the **Set as default printer** option from the drop-down menu.

Once you have installed and configured your printers, the quickest way to print a simple document or file is to print using Windows itself. Locate the file that you want to print in a folder, maybe **Documents**, right-click it, and select **Print**. Windows will print it using your default printer settings.

For more control of the print operation, you should open the document in a program and use its **File**, **Print** menu options.

Managing Print Jobs

If you want to find out what is happening when you have sent documents to your printer, double-click the **See what's printing** option in the Printer Control window, or double-click the printer icon 🖶 in the Notification Area of the Task bar, to open the **Print Queue**.

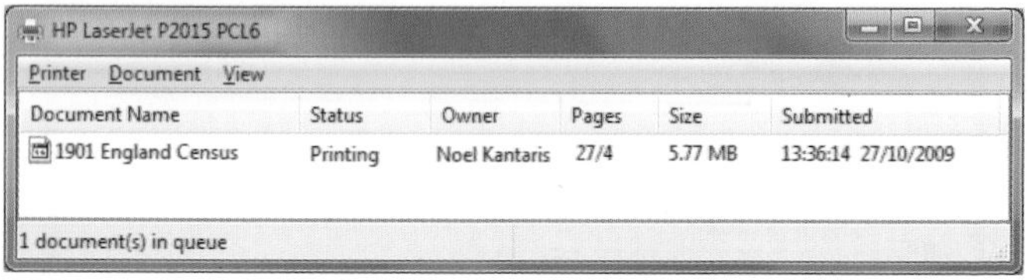

Fig. 7.12 The Print Queue

This displays detailed information about the work actually being printed, or of print jobs that are waiting in the queue. This includes the name of the document, its status and 'owner', when it was added to the print queue, the printing progress and when printing was started.

You can control the printing operations from the **Printer** and **Document** menu options of the **Print Queue** window. Selecting **Printer**, **Pause Printing** will stop the operation until you make the same selection again. The **Cancel All Documents** option will remove all the print jobs from the queue, but it sometimes takes a while.

The Windows Fax and Scan Utility

Windows 7 ships with a Fax and Scan utility which actually works. The Scan part of the utility has always worked in previous versions of Windows, but for us this is the first version of Windows which successfully addresses Faxes, ironically as they are losing their popularity!

To use the Fax utility, all you have to do is to connect your PC's Fax modem to a telephone line, but remember that if you are on Broadband this connection has to be made via a Broadband filter.

To start the Fax and Scan utility, either double-click the **Fax** icon ≅ in the **Devices and Printers** folder, or click the **Start** button 🌐 then click the **Windows Fax and Scan** entry in the **All Programs** list. Both open the window below.

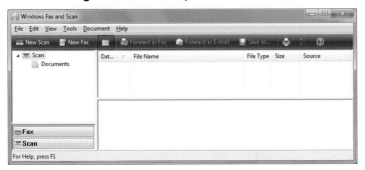

Fig. 7.13 The Opening Fax and Scan Utility Window

As you can see from the opening screen of this utility, you can select either a **New Scan** or a **New Fax**. Clicking the **New Fax** button, opens the window below.

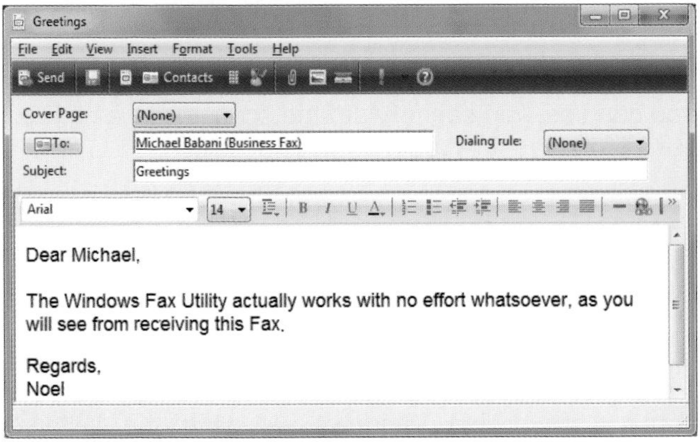

Fig. 7.14 The New Fax Screen

Note that the Fax utility is very similar to an e-mail program. You can select the recipient from your contacts list, provided you have a separate entry for the Fax number, you can attach a file, etc. We find that in terms of readability, the best font size for the body of the Fax is 14 point.

Next, click the **New Scan** button (see Fig. 7.13) to open the first Scan screen in which you can change the Resolution, Brightness and Contrast of your scanner, and Preview or Scan the object in question. Pressing the Scan button, opens the window below.

Fig. 7.15 The New Scan Screen

As you can see, you can forward the scan image as a Fax, as an e-mail, or save it. A really wonderful utility!

Working with Programs

Installing programs on your PC is very easy with Windows 7. Just place the CD or DVD that the software came on in the appropriate drive and Windows will start the installation process automatically. If you downloaded the program from the Internet, it should run and install itself.

Clicking the **Programs** section of the **Control Panel** opens the sub-panel shown in Fig. 7.16.

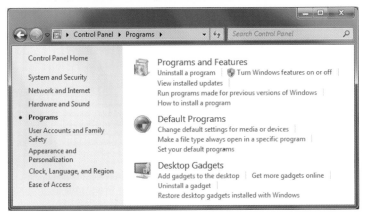

Fig. 7.16 The Programs Section of the Control Panel

Uninstall or Change a Program

Uninstalling programs or changing an already installed one is very easy with Windows. To do either, click the **Uninstall a program** link in the **Programs and Features** section of the **Control Panel**, shown in Fig. 7.16 above, to open a colourful window similar to the one in Fig. 7.17 on the next page. Your contents will not be the same, obviously!

After selecting a program the four options, **Organize**, **Uninstall**, **Change**, and **Repair**, may appear on the toolbar, as shown in Fig. 7.17. With some programs **Change** and/or **Repair** are not available, while with others **Change** is replaced by the **Repair** option.

Using the option to **Uninstall** a program, removes all trace of it from your hard disc, although sometimes the folders are left empty on your hard drive.

Note: Be careful with this application, because double-clicking a program on the list might remove it without further warning!

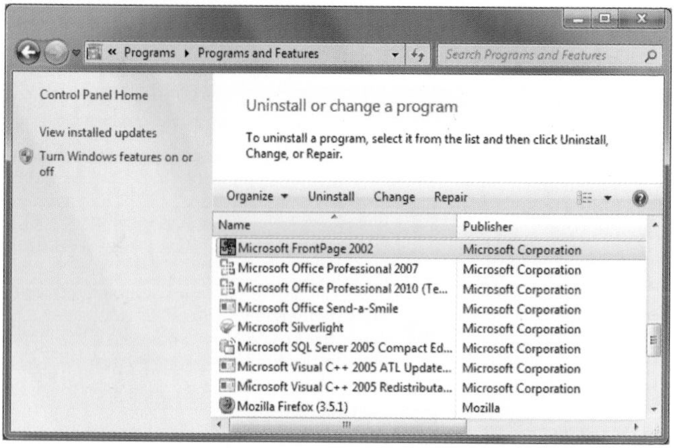

Fig. 7.17 Uninstalling and Changing Programs

Windows Features

Some programs and features included with Windows, must be turned on before you can use them, and others such as Internet Explorer 8, can be turned off. Some are turned on by default, but you can turn them off if you don't need them.

Fig. 7.18 Windows Features

You might not need to make any changes to your Windows 7 features, but if you do, just click the **Turn Windows features on or off** link in the **Programs and Features** section of the **Control Panel** (Fig. 7.16), to open the Windows Features box shown in Fig. 7.18 above. Here you can select the features you want included with Windows by ticking in the boxes.

8

Accessibility

 The **Ease of Access Center** lets you change settings to make your PC more accessible for people who have visual or hearing difficulties, suffer pain in their hands or arms and/or have other reasoning and cognitive issues.

The easiest way to open the **Ease of Access Center** is the ⊞**+U** keyboard shortcut. A longer way is the **Control Panel**, **Ease of Access, Ease of Access Center** command sequence. Both methods open the window shown in Fig. 8.1.

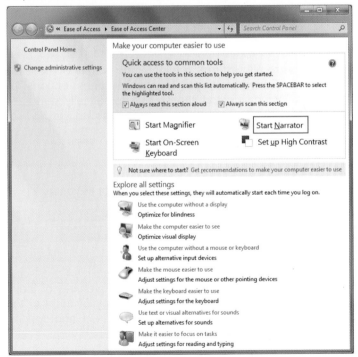

Fig. 8.1 The Ease of Access Center

The **Ease of Access Center** includes a quick access panel at the top with a highlight rotating through the four most common tools; **Magnifier**, **Narrator**, **On-Screen Keyboard**, and **High Contrast**. A voice, the Narrator, also tells you what option is selected. Pressing the **Spacebar** on a highlighted option will start it for you.

If the Narrator annoys you, click the **Always read this section aloud** box to remove the tick mark from it. While you are doing this, you could also remove the tick mark from the **Always scan this section** box, to stop the focus from rotating between the four entries.

The 💡 **Get recommendations...** link opens a five-stage questionnaire. Depending on your answers to questions about performing routine tasks, such as whether you have difficulty seeing faces or text on TV, hearing conversations, or using a pen or pencil, Windows 7 will provide a recommendation of the accessibility settings and programs that are likely to improve your ability to see, hear, and use your computer. This has to be a good place to start.

The **Explore all settings** section at the bottom of the **Ease of Access Center** lets you explore settings options by categories. When selected, these will automatically start each time you log on to the computer. They include:

- Using the computer without a display
- Making the computer easier to see
- Using the computer without a mouse or keyboard
- Changing mouse or keyboard settings
- Using text or visual alternatives for sounds
- Making it easier to focus on tasks.

In the next few pages we will give you an overview of these various options, but we will not discuss any of them in too much detail, as different people have different and specific needs!

The Microsoft Magnifier

To start the Magnifier, click on **Start Magnifier** (words not icon) shown in Fig. 8.1.

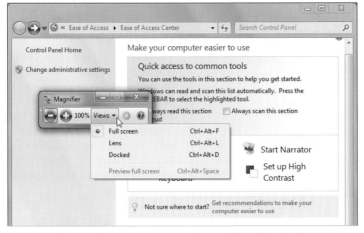

Fig. 8.2 Computer Screen with the Magnifier Active

The new Magnifier window has two views: **Full screen** (the default as shown above), and **Lens**, selected from the **Views** drop-down list shown open in Fig. 8.2. In **Lens** view, wherever you place the mouse pointer the screen is magnified. The Magnifier window allows you to increase ● or decrease ● the magnification, or use the Options icon ● to turn on colour inversion, select tracking options and fine-tune screen fonts.

 If you don't use the Magnifier window for more than a few seconds, it turns into an actual magnifying glass icon, as shown here. Clicking this Magnifier icon again, re-opens the Magnifier window shown in Fig. 8.2.

To close down the Magnifier, click the **Close** button in the Magnifier window.

This feature takes a while to get used to, but it can be well worthwhile trying it out.

Microsoft Narrator

Narrator is a basic screen reader built into Windows and may be useful for the visually impaired. It reads dialogue boxes and window controls in a number of Windows basic applications, as long as the computer being used has a sound card and speakers or headphones.

Fig. 8.3 Microsoft Narrator

To open it, click the **Start Narrator** option in the **Ease of Access Center** (Fig. 8.1). Anna will start speaking in an electronic voice and the Microsoft Narrator window will open, as shown in Fig. 8.3. This is where you can customise and control the **Narrator**.

If you find this facility useful you will need to play around with the **Main Narrator Settings** until you get it working the best way for you. To close **Narrator** just click the **Exit** button.

The On-Screen Keyboard

To activate the **On-Screen Keyboard** (Fig. 8.4), click the **Start On-Screen Keyboard** option in the **Ease of Access Center** shown earlier in Fig. 8.1.

Fig. 8.4 The On-Screen Keyboard

This excellent new virtual keyboard opens on the screen and allows users with mobility impairments to type data using a mouse pointer, a joystick, or other pointing device. The result is exactly as if you were using the actual keyboard. It has three typing modes selected when the **Options** key is clicked. These are:

Clicking mode – you click the on-screen keys to type text.

Hovering mode – you use a mouse or joystick to point to a key for a predefined period of time, and the selected character is typed automatically.

Scanning mode – the **On-Screen Keyboard** continually scans the keyboard and highlights areas where you can type keyboard characters by pressing a hot key or using a switch-input device.

You can also adjust the settings for your 'physical' keyboard by clicking the ⬛ **Make the keyboard easier to use** entry at the bottom of the **Ease of Access Center** window, and selecting various options on the displayed window.

Turn on Mouse Keys lets you move the mouse pointer by pressing the arrow keys on the keyboard's numeric pad.

Turn on Sticky Keys allows you to press the **Ctrl**, **Alt**, and **Shift**, keys one at a time, instead of all at the same time. This is useful for people who have difficulty pressing two or more keys at a time.

Turn on Toggle Keys makes your PC play a high-pitched sound when the **Caps Lock**, **Scroll Lock**, or **Num Lock** keys are used. The **Turn on Filter Keys** option tells the keyboard to ignore brief or repeated keystrokes.

The Display Options

To make your screen easier to see you can try the **Set up High Contrast** option in Fig. 8.1. This opens a window in which you can set programs to change their colour-specific schemes to a **High Contrast** scheme, change the size of text, set the thickness of the blinking cursor, etc.

The Mouse Options

Clicking the ✏ **Make the mouse easier to use** link at the bottom of Fig. 8.1, displays the window below.

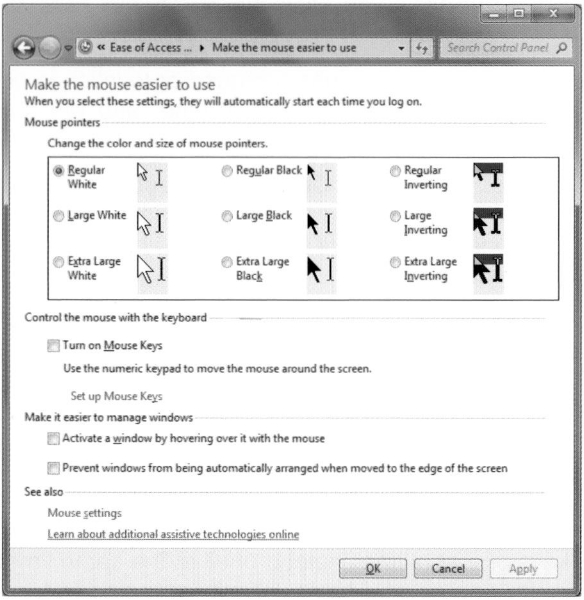

Fig. 8.5 Making the Mouse Easier to Use

Here you can change the colour and size of the mouse pointer, and control the mouse pointer's movements with the keys on the numeric keypad.

Clicking the **Set up Mouse Keys** link, displays an additional window in which you can control, amongst other things, the speed at which the mouse pointer moves, and the shortcut key combination you need to activate and deactivate the numeric keypad.

* * *

We leave it to you to explore the other settings on the list in the lower half of the **Ease of Access Center**. It is the only way of finding out what suits you personally. Good luck!

Index